# JesusWalk®
# Beginning the Journey
## Discipleship and Spiritual Formation Lessons
OR
A Curriculum for Training and Mentoring New Believers in
Christian Doctrines, Core Values, and Spiritual Disciplines

by Dr. Ralph F. Wilson
JesusWalk® Bible Study Series

Free online videos of this series are available at:
www.jesuswalk.com/beginning/

DVDs, additional books, and reprint licenses are available at:
www.jesuswalk.com/books/beginning.htm

Free Participant Guide handout sheets are available at:
www.jesuswalk.com/beginning/beginning-handouts.pdf

JesusWalk® Publications
Loomis, California

Paperback
ISBN-13:         978-0-9819721-1-4
ISBN-10:         098197211X


Library of Congress Control Number: 2009932275

**Library of Congress subject headings:**
Spiritual formation
Discipleship essentials
Discipleship Resources
Discipling (Christianity)
Christian life—Biblical teaching
Christian life—Study and teaching


Published by JesusWalk® Publications, P.O. Box 565, Loomis, CA 95650-0565, USA.

JesusWalk is a registered trademark and Joyful Heart is a trademark of Joyful Heart Renewal Ministries.

Unless otherwise noted, all the Bible verses quoted are from the New International Version (International Bible Society, 1973, 1978), used by permission.

# Introduction

If you have just become a follower of Jesus, congratulations! You have begun the most important journey of your life!

We have designed these lessons to help you begin the journey well. Just as you might go to an outdoor or wilderness store to outfit yourself for a hike in the mountains, these lessons will equip you for the early stages of your Christian journey.

The Christian life deserves the best start you can give it.

## A Journey with Others

Let me begin with a basic assumption. The "Jesus walk" is not a solitary journey, but one undertaken with Jesus himself *and* some of his disciples. If you try to do this study by yourself, you will miss out. That is because many of the secrets of the Christian life are not just taught, they are caught as they are modeled in the lives of other believers.

If you are planning to go on a backpacking trip, you may get all the books you can on the subject. But it is even better to go on a hike with an experienced person who has been on the trail before.

## Getting Started

In this series, we look at 12 basic lessons on living as a Christ follower. We examine Christianity from three points of view so you get a well-rounded introduction.

1. **Beliefs**—What we believe about God's grace through Jesus, the Father, and the Holy Spirit, known as "doctrine."
2. **Values**—The radical principles that Jesus teaches us concerning love, forgiveness, generosity, and service.
3. **Spiritual Disciplines**—How to live the Christian life successfully: prayer, resisting temptation, worship, and living by the Holy Spirit.

Each of these is important to help you grow healthy as a Christ-follower. You'll learn how to be a disciple. The mandate for discipleship comes from Jesus' command: "Make disciples of all nations" (Matthew 28:19) – that is, committed learners and followers. This process also involves spiritual formation, that is, character development patterned after Christ himself, as St. Paul put it, "I am again in the pains of childbirth until Christ is formed in you" (Galatians 4:19).

## How these Lessons Work

Here are the components of the *JesusWalk: Beginning the Journey* experience:

1.  **Mentor.** These lessons are intended to be studied with a mentor, a person who has been a Christian for a while. The word "mentor" means, "a trusted counselor or guide; tutor, coach." One of the most important functions of your mentor is to help you develop healthy habits of Christian living and provide accountability so you will grow steadily and well. Do not try to do this alone.
2.  **Meeting Weekly.** Over the course of this study, you will be meeting each week with your mentor. Of course, it is possible to read all the lessons in a few hours. But learning to live as a Christian is not primarily understanding a set of beliefs. Rather it involves internalizing a lifestyle of following Jesus in a personal way. This is a process that takes time—hence, the weekly lessons.
3.  **Lessons.** The teaching portion of each lesson is available on the Internet in video, audio, and written form at no charge. If you are able, try to watch the video together with your mentor. If, for some reason, the video is not available, then listen to the audio together or read the lesson aloud together. Video and audio lessons are at:

    www.jesuswalk.com/beginning

4.  **Questions and Discussion Points.** After you watch or listen to the lesson, then talk about each of the questions and discussion points with your mentor. The questions will help you understand better the important points of the lesson. Other discussion points are opportunities for you and your mentor to talk about different aspects of Christian life.
5.  **Bible Memory Verse.** Memorization of one verse each lesson helps the new believer internalize the truths of that lesson.

By design, these 12 lessons are quite basic. If you have been a Christian for a while, you'll probably find them too simple for you. You need Bible studies that are more challenging. But if you're a new Christian—especially if you don't have a Christian background—you'll find these lessons are just what you need to help you grow in Christ.

## How to Find a Mentor

Often a church will help find a mentor for new Christians. If so, you don't have to worry about it. But if you are a new Christian who does *not* have a mentor, here are some ways to find one:

1.  **Pray and ask God** to help you find a mentor who can meet with you. God is faithful and will answer your prayers.

2. **Invite a Christian** whom you know and respect to be your mentor for these lessons. Even if *this* person is not able to help you, he or she may be able to find you a mentor who can meet with you. Then have this person read or watch the video in Appendix 1, "The Role of the Mentor."

3. **Ask the pastor** of a church near where you live. The pastor may not be familiar with *JesusWalk: Beginning the Journey* materials, so you might want to bring with you some pages that you have printed out. The pastor can probably find a person in the church who can help you. Be sure to have the pastor read or watch the video in Appendix 2, "For Pastors and Church Leaders."

## A Desire to Learn

You may want to jump ahead in the lessons. That is a natural desire. But remember, this is a process of spiritual formation in your soul, not a body of material to be mastered for a written test. You can look ahead, but for this series to produce actual spiritual growth in you—rather than just increase your knowledge—you need to watch the video (or read the material) *and discuss it with your mentor each week.* You'll get *much more* out of it this way!

## Get Started

Once you have found a mentor, make an appointment to get together for your first meeting. It will be the beginning of a great relationship that will help you on your journey.

If you haven't already, do me a favor a register online for the course.

www.jesuswalk.com/contact/beginning-registration.htm

There's no charge, but it will allow me to send you my periodic *Joyful Heart Newsletter* that will let you know about other Bible studies as they become available. May God richly bless you as you learn to walk with Christ!

Yours in Christ's service,
Dr. Ralph F. Wilson

# Table of Contents

# Reprint Guidelines

**Copying the Handouts**. In some cases, small groups or Sunday school classes would like to use the Participant Guide handouts. That's great. An online file provides copies of the handouts designed for classes and small groups. There is no charge whatsoever to print out as many copies of the handouts as you need for participants. They can be found at:

www.jesuswalk.com/beginning/beginning-handouts.pdf

All charts and notes are copyrighted and must bear the line:

"Copyright © 2009, Ralph F. Wilson. All rights reserved. Reprinted by permission."

You may not resell these notes to other groups or individuals outside your congregation. You may, however, charge people in your group enough to cover your copying costs.

**Copying the book (or the majority of it).** If you copy the book for your congregation or group, you are requested to purchase a reprint license for each book. For better copies, I recommend that you reprint the e-book version, not the paperback version. A Reprint License, $2.50 for each copy, is available for purchase at:

www.jesuswalk.com/books/beginning.htm

Or you may send a check to:

>    Dr. Ralph F. Wilson
>    JesusWalk Publications
>    PO Box 565
>    Loomis, CA 95650, USA

The Scripture says,

>    "The laborer is worthy of his hire" (Luke 10:7) and "Anyone who receives instruction in
>    the word must share all good things with his instructor" (Galatians 6:6).

However, if you are from a third world country or an area where it is difficult to transmit money, please make a small contribution instead to help the poor in your community.

# 1. Rescue—Grace and Forgiveness

You have become a new Christian. Congratulations! This step is the most important one you will make in your whole life.

Exactly what has happened? It depends upon your point of view. Unless they too are believers, your family and friends may think you've "got religion" or may imagine that you are crazy. Your Christian friends are probably overjoyed that you have decided to follow Christ. And you? You may have all sorts of thoughts and emotions flooding through you—joy, wonder, anxiety, enthusiasm, freedom—or perhaps no emotions at all. That is okay. We are all different.

## Jesus and the Lost Sheep

A story that Jesus told can help explain what has happened to you. Since Jesus grew up in a rural culture, many of the stories he told—known as "parables"—were about raising crops and herding animals. He told this famous story about a shepherd:

> "Suppose one of you has a hundred sheep and loses one of them. Does he not leave the ninety-nine in the open country and go after the lost sheep until he finds it? And when he finds it, he joyfully puts it on his shoulders and goes home. Then he calls his friends and neighbors together and says, 'Rejoice with me; I have found my lost sheep.' I tell you that in the same way there will be more rejoicing in heaven over one sinner who repents[1] than over ninety-nine righteous persons who don't need to repent." (Luke 15:4-7)

At the close of each day a shepherd would count his flock of sheep as he brought them into the sheepfold for protection at night. The shepherd discovers that one sheep was missing. He goes out into the hills to find the missing sheep. Perhaps the sheep doesn't even realize it is lost or in danger. But the shepherd knows that if he does not find it, a predator will probably kill it by morning. So the shepherd searches. He calls out the sheep's name in the dark, listens for its bleating, and does not give up. When he finally finds the sheep, he rejoices. He puts the sheep over his shoulders and comes home with joy.

---

[1] "Repent" means to be sorry for sin and to turn away from it.

You are like the sheep in the parable. The Good Shepherd has been searching for you. You were lost, alone, going the wrong way. If Jesus had not found you and rescued you, where would you be?

But he loves you and cares about you—so much, that at great effort he rescued you and brought you to safety.

## Rescued = Saved

I tell this story because Christians sometimes explain what has happened on your life with the words "saved" and "salvation." These words mean "rescued"—rescued from danger of being separated from the Shepherd forever, rescued from sin, rescued from punishment, rescued from meaninglessness. When Christians say "you are saved," they mean that Jesus has found you and rescued you from a life that was in grave danger of harm.

One way to think about your new life as a Christian is as having been "rescued" or "saved." Let me explain three more ways to understand your relationship to God—loved, forgiven, accepted. These concepts will anchor your faith.

## Loved

The first concept is: You are loved by God. In these lessons, I'll be introducing various Bible verses that teach these concepts. Here is one:

> "For God so loved the world that he gave his one and only Son, that whoever believes in him shall not perish but have eternal life." (John 3:16)

God loves you—you personally. Christianity at its very core is based on love. God's love for you. Jesus' love for you. Because God loved you so much, he sent Jesus to this world to rescue you and give you eternal life with him. You are loved—no matter what you have done and no matter what you might do in the future.

## Forgiven

The second concept is: You are forgiven by God. Jesus died on the cross for your sins. When you became a Christian, you probably told God about the sins that you have committed and asked his forgiveness. Know this: God has forgiven you. The Bible says:

> "If we confess our sins, he is faithful and just and will forgive us our sins and purify us from all unrighteousness." (1 John 1:9)

Forgiven means that God does not hold your sin against you any longer. Yes, you committed sins, but they have been forgiven. God does not hold a grudge against you.

But what if you sin again after becoming a Christian? What then?

You probably *will* sin in the future—many times. But the same idea applies. Confess your sin to God and he will forgive you, again and again! We will consider this more deeply in Lesson 3. But know this: You are forgiven! That is the way God looks at you.

## Accepted

The third important concept is: God accepts you. You don't have to do something good to be accepted. He accepts you just as you are.

If you are a parent, then you understand this. You don't say to your child:

"I will not accept you as my son until you are completely potty trained." OR

"I will not accept you as my daughter until you learn to walk without falling down."

That is silly. Parents accept their children just as they are from the day they are born. They don't expect an infant to walk or be potty trained. They accept the baby just as he is or she is. They know that as the baby grows, he will finally become potty trained. She will finally learn to walk. She is not accepted *because* she walks. Children are accepted by parents for who they are, without having to achieve anything.

God is your Father who accepts you just as you are. He loves you, and as you grow, he will help you to become more and more like him. He does not accept you on the basis of your being able to avoid sin, but because he has found you, loved you, and forgiven you.

It is really rather amazing and wonderful!

## Grace and Mercy

Let me introduce two more words that will help you understand what happened to you when you became a Christian—grace and mercy.

- **Grace** is the favor that God decides to show you, unrelated to anything you might do to deserve it. Grace is about God's love toward you, not about your worthiness.
- **Mercy** is not getting the punishment you deserve.

One of the most wonderful verses in the Bible explains what happened to you when you became a Christian. It is a verse worth memorizing and thinking deeply about:

"For it is by grace you have been saved, through faith—and this not from yourselves, it is the gift of God— not by works, so that no one can boast." (Ephesians 2:8-9)

It is because of God's grace—his amazing love and favor towards you—that you have been saved or rescued. It is like a gift. You did not do anything to deserve it. The only thing you did was to have "faith," that is, trust in Jesus. You believed that he loved you and would help you. That is it!

You did not deserve God's grace. In fact, you deserved the opposite for a life of going your own way in a kind of passive (or active) rebellion against God. So when you think about being "found" and "rescued," know that God did this because he wanted to, not because you were so worthy or so good.

This is important. You will probably sin and then think: I am terrible. Because I keep on sinning, God will not love me. The only way I can get God to love me is to be perfect.

Believe me, this is a lie that says you will never be loved, because you will never be perfect.

The good news is that you were rescued, loved, forgiven, and accepted, not because you deserved it. So you can't lose God's love because you sin. He loves you -- period!

That is what grace is.

One of my favorite Christian songs, "Amazing Grace," was written by a person who was once a truly evil man. John Newton was the cruel captain of ships that transported slaves from Africa to America. Then he became a Christian. God helped him gradually to change. Finally he became a preacher who helped stop the slave trade in the entire British Empire. Looking back on his terrible past, he wrote these immortal words:

> "Amazing grace, how sweet the sound
> That saved a wretch like me.
> I once was lost, but now I'm found.
> Was blind, but now I see."

## Baptism

Before we leave this lesson, let us talk about baptism. Baptism is a sacrament or ordinance, that is, a sacred act that is a sign or symbol of what God has done in your life. When people come to believe in Jesus, one of the first things they want to do is to be baptized as a way of saying: "I belong to Jesus."

Jesus commanded his disciples in the Great Commission:

> "Therefore go and make disciples of all nations, **baptizing them in the name of the Father and of the Son and of the Holy Spirit**, and teaching them to obey everything I have commanded you. And surely I am with you always, to the very end of the age." (Matthew 28:19-20)

We are baptized because this is what Jesus instructed. Let me briefly explain what baptism means.

### 1. Baptism is a sign that you are united with Jesus

When you are baptized as a Christian, people understand that you are identifying yourself solidly with Jesus. In fact, the Bible mentions this as a way of uniting yourself to Jesus (Romans 6:5). It is more than symbolic. There is something spiritual going on that is hard to put into words.

### 2. Baptism is a sign that your sins are washed away

The water used in baptism is a symbol of cleansing. When you finally became a Christian, you accepted the fact that Jesus has forgiven your sins. Baptism is an outward way of symbolizing what has happened inside of you.

### 3. Baptism is a sign of commitment to a new Master

Baptism is a sign that you have committed yourself, your life, to a new Master. Baptism is not a mark of pride, so much as a mark of humility and submission to Christ.

Men are often hesitant to commit themselves to marriage. Why? Because they know that when they say the marriage vows, they take on responsibilities. In the same way, some people are hesitant to be baptized, because they are afraid of commitment. They put it off. They are like people who want the joys of marriage without the commitment.

Now that you are a Christian, you will want to talk to a pastor about how to be baptized. The pastor will guide you in what to do next.

In this lesson, we have talked about being rescued, saved, loved, accepted, and forgiven. We have explored God's grace and mercy towards us, and how we respond to these through faith and baptism.

Christianity is based on a simple but profound truth: **God loves you! Believe it!**

## Prayer

Thank you, Lord, for loving me. Thank you for forgiving my sins. I don't deserve what you have given me. I can only offer my faith and thanks in return. In Jesus' name, I pray. Amen.

## Participant Guide: 1. Rescue—Grace and Forgiveness

### Memory Verse

"For it is by grace you have been saved, through faith--and this not from yourselves, it is the gift of God—not by works, so that no one can boast." (Ephesians 2:8-9, NIV)

### Questions and Discussion Points

1. **Talk about** what Jesus rescued you from. In what way were you like the lost sheep in the story in Luke 15:4-7?

2. **Discuss** why you believe that God loves you. Does he love you because you are loveable or good? Does he accept you only if you meet certain conditions?

3. **Discuss** how you know you have been forgiven. Based on 1 John 1:9, if you sin after becoming a Christian, can you be cleansed from your sins again? What does it mean to "confess" your sins to God?

4. **Discuss** why so many people think they have to be good to earn God's favor. Based on Ephesians 2:8-9, is there any way to earn God's favor? What is the place of faith or trust in this process?

5. **Sing** (if you know the tune) the first verse of "Amazing Grace." Why do you think John Newton was so thankful for God's grace?

6. **Ask** your mentor when he or she was baptized and to tell you how it happened.

7. **Find out** how to be baptized in the church or group you have been attending.

8. **Make an appointment** to talk to the pastor or group leader about being baptized.

9. **Read the memory verse**, Ephesians 2:8-9 five times aloud with your mentor—even though it may seem a bit silly doing it. Then write it on a 3" x 5" card. (Any size will do.) That is how you begin to memorize something. Each lesson will have a memory verse that contains such an important truth that it is worth the time and effort to memorize.

10. **Pray together** about your new life in Christ. If you are not very comfortable praying aloud yet, ask your mentor to pray for you.

11. **Appointment**. Set a time and place to meet to go through next week's lesson.

## Outline of Lesson 1. Rescue—Grace and Forgiveness

1. **You are a new Christian. What happened to you?**
   - God has rescued you.
   - Jesus' Parable of the Lost Sheep (Luke 15:4-7)
     - Jesus rescues us like the shepherd in the story rescued the endangered, straying sheep.
     - In Christian jargon "saved" means rescued.
   - God loves you (John 3:16).
   - God has forgiven you.
   - Jesus died on the cross for your sins.
     - There is a promise of forgiveness in 1 John 1:9.
     - Forgiveness means that God doesn't hold your sin against you.
     - In the future, if you sin, confess your sins and God will forgive you.
   - God accepts you unconditionally as his child. You don't have to do anything to earn acceptance.

2. **God shows you grace and mercy**
   - "Grace" is God's favor to you, which you don't deserve and can't earn (Ephesians 2:8-9).
   - "Mercy" is not getting the punishment you deserve.
   - Song: "Amazing Grace" was written by ex-slave ship captain John Newton, who experienced God's grace.

3. **Baptism**
   - In the Great Commission, Jesus commanded us to be baptized (Matthew 28:19-20).
   - Baptism is a sign:
     - That you are united with Jesus.
     - That your sins are washed away.
     - Of your commitment to a new Master.
   - Talk to a pastor about being baptized.

# 2. Disciple—Following Jesus Daily

Jesus had a way of calling people to follow him. Picture this scene:

> "As Jesus was walking beside the Sea of Galilee, he saw two brothers, Simon called Peter and his brother Andrew. They were casting a net into the lake, for they were fishermen. 'Come, follow me,' Jesus said, 'and I will make you fishers of men.' At once they left their nets and followed him." (Matthew 4:18-20)

Jesus has called you, too. You have begun the journey to follow Jesus. How do you nurture this new relationship so that it grows stronger and richer rather than becoming stagnant? In this lesson, we will talk about several ways to grow in your relationship to Christ: through your own self-image, through reading the Bible, and through prayer.

## The Disciple Concept

Part of being a follower of Jesus is the way you think about and understand yourself in relation to Jesus. Here are some common terms that describe this:

- **Christian** means, literally, "little Christ." It refers to people who identify themselves with Christ's teaching and lifestyle. Unfortunately, "Christian" has been defined so broadly that it is sometimes used to refer to people who are not serious about putting their faith into practice.
- **Believer** is a great word. It talks about putting your faith and trust in Jesus.
- **Disciple** is the term used in the Bible to describe Christ followers. Literally, "disciple" means, "learner." It refers to those who have left their former way of life to follow Jesus and learn from him, who have a trust in him and a commitment to follow his teachings.
- **Christ-follower or Jesus-follower** indicates a committed follower of Christ. The big advantage of these terms is that they are understood positively by our culture, yet with clarity, to describe a person who identifies strongly with Jesus.

Since you have decided to follow Jesus, I encourage you to think of yourself as a Christian, a believer, a disciple, a Christ-follower. You are someone who is really committed to walk Jesus' path and learn from him.

Your understanding of yourself, your self-image, has a lot to do with how you will live out this commitment.

## Read the Bible Daily

Following Jesus as his disciple means learning from him so that your life begins to conform itself to his teaching and value system. Since Jesus is not here in the flesh, the best way to learn from Jesus is to read his teachings in the Bible.

I realize that the Bible is a foreign book to many, so let me explain some basics.

The Bible has two parts:

1. **Old Testament** is the part of the Bible written before Christ, literally "B.C." It explains how God revealed himself to ancient followers of God, such as Abraham, Moses, and the various prophets.

2. **New Testament** is the part of the Bible that records Jesus' own teachings, provides a history of how Christianity spread in the earliest days, and includes instructive letters written by Jesus' authorized spokesmen—his apostles. I recommend that you start with the New Testament first, then read the Old Testament later.

In particular, I recommend that you begin your reading of the New Testament in the Gospels, which tell the story of Jesus' life. They appear right at the beginning of the New Testament. The Gospel of Mark or the Gospel of John is a great place to start.

If you have a Bible already, great! If not, ask your mentor for guidance on how to get a Bible. Some churches give a Bible to a new Christian. You can also find a Bible at a Christian bookstore. I have two recommendations here:

1. **Get a newer translation**, one translated in the last 50 years. You will find it much easier to read and understand.

2. **Get a study Bible**, one with footnotes that explain different aspects of what you are reading.

For more information on this, see Lesson 11, Bible—Guidebook for Living and Appendix 3, How to Select a Bible.

## Chapters and Verses

In these lessons you will see Bible references like this: Heb. 4:12. Let me explain. Heb. is an abbreviation for Hebrews, a book in the New Testament. You will find its location by looking it up in the Table of Contents in the front of your Bible, which will show the page number on which Hebrews begins. The numbers 4:12 refer to the chapter and verse. Books are divided into chapters—this would be chapter 4. Each chapter has many verses, usually only a sentence or two long. This refers to verse 12 of chapter 4 in the book of Hebrews.

## Learning to Pray

Besides reading the Bible, you will want to pray each day. Praying is talking directly to God. Some people seem to use very formal and eloquent words in their prayers. This can be very intimidating to a new Christian. The good news is that God wants you to pray in your *own* words. He wants you to talk to him about what is going on in your life.

Some people think that prayer is asking God for things—a pretty selfish basis for a relationship. That is only part of prayer. Prayer is much broader than that. Let me give you an easy way to remember how you can pray:

## ACTS

ACTS is an acronym that can remind you of different kinds of prayer—even a good order in which to pray to God.

### Adoration

"A" stands for Adoration, that is, offering words of love and praise to God. If you are married or have a boyfriend or girlfriend, then you know how important it is to say, "I love you." Many Christian songs involve telling God how much we love him. It is a great way to begin our prayers.

### Confession

"C" stands for Confession, that is, telling God about our sins, rather than pretending that we are perfect. In prayer we ask God to help us not to sin and ask for forgiveness.

### Thanksgiving

"T" stands for Thanksgiving, that is, thanking God for all the things he has done for us. Thanksgiving puts us in a proper frame of mind to be able to ask for things later without being either greedy or unbelieving. God supplies our needs and deserves our thanks.

### Supplication

"S" stands for Supplication, a word that means "asking for something." For many people, prayer is *only* asking for help and things we need. That is important, but, as we have seen, it should be only one part of our prayer. By all means, when you have problems, bring them to God. Tell God about what you are feeling. Establish this line of communication. If you have needs, ask God to meet them for you. Remember, however, that God is not our errand boy, but our Father, the Creator of the universe. We don't order him about, but with love and trust we bring our needs to him.

## Set Aside a "Quiet Time"

I encourage you to set aside a time every day when you can spend some time reading the Bible, praying, and listening to God. Five to ten minutes each day is a good place to start. It is hard to begin this kind of new habit, but you will find it will help you a great deal to grow as a Christian. In fact, I have found that Christians who don't spend this kind of quiet time with God often end up stunted, immature—kind of like overgrown babies.

But don't confine your prayers only to this quiet time. Talk to God throughout the day, whenever you think of him. Gradually, you will find that you can live every hour of your life conscious of him and in touch with him. And that is the point of being a Jesus-follower.

## Ask for Guidance

At the beginning of each day, ask God to guide you through that day. Ask him to direct your steps, guide your actions, and to keep you from temptation.

Then spend some time in quiet, listening. One wonderful truth is that God can speak to our hearts and guide us if we will be quiet before him.

As you read Jesus' teachings, you will understand better his values and his lifestyle. Then, when you come to a situation that you are not sure what to do, ask: "What would Jesus do?" To answer this question with accuracy, of course, we must know Jesus' teachings and life. But it is a great question through which God can guide us.

Following Jesus in our day is not a physical following as it was for Jesus' first disciples. Rather, it is a deliberate, spiritual following, through:

1.  Seeing ourselves as Christ's followers,
2.  Reading Jesus' teachings in the Bible,
3.  Praying to him often, and
4.  Seeking his guidance.

This is how we start the journey.

## Prayer

Lord, I have begun to follow you. Help me to think of myself every day as your disciple. Teach me more as I build this relationship through reading the Bible and prayer. I don't know where this journey with you will lead, Jesus, but I am trusting and following you. In your name, I pray. Amen.

## Participant Guide: 2. Disciple—Following Jesus Daily

### Memory Verse

"To the Jews who had believed him, Jesus said, 'If you hold to my teaching, you are really my disciples. Then you will know the truth, and the truth will set you free.'" (John 8:31-32, NIV)

### Questions and Discussion Points

1.  **Read aloud five times** the new memory verse (John 8:31-32) and write it on a card.
2.  **Discuss** why it is important how you think of your relationship to God. How will an understanding of yourself as a "disciple," a "Christ-follower," or a "Jesus-follower" help change your actions?
3.  **Discuss.** How you would describe your relationship to God to someone who did not have the same kind of belief in Jesus that you now have?
4.  **Look in** the front of a Bible to locate the Table of Contents. Here is where you can find the page numbers of the books contained in the Bible.
5.  **Find** the two main parts of the Bible. Do you remember what they are called?
6.  **Find** the four Gospels (Matthew, Mark, Luke, and John) and the book of Acts, all in the New Testament.
7.  **Decide** which Gospel you will begin to read each day. (Recommendation: John or Mark)
8.  **Locate and read** Hebrews 4:12 in your Bible.
9.  **Discuss** how you can obtain a Bible of your own, if you don't have one already.
10. **Plan** the time of the day in which you will set aside 5 or 10 minutes to read your Bible and pray. This should be a time that you are awake and, if possible, a time that you can set aside nearly every day.
11. **Say from memory** (or try to) last lesson's memory verse: Ephesians 2:8-9. If you can't say it flawlessly yet, take out the card you wrote it on, read it, then try to say it again from memory.
12. **Pray together** about your new life in Christ and any problems you are currently having.
13. **Appointment.** Set a time and place to meet and go through next week's lesson.

## Outline of Lesson 2. Disciple—Following Jesus Daily

1. **The disciple concept impacts your self-image**
   - Jesus called Peter and Andrew. They left their nets and followed him (Matthew 4:18-20).
   - "Christian" means "little Christ," a reference to Christ's followers, but is used too broadly in our day.
   - "Believer" emphasizes putting your faith in Christ.
   - "Disciple" means "learner," used of the early followers of Jesus.
   - "Christ-follower" or "Jesus-follower" refers to a committed follower of Christ, a term understood positively in our culture.

2. **Read the Bible Daily**
   - Bible reading helps you learn Jesus' teachings directly
   - The Bible has two parts: Old Testament and New Testament
   - Begin with the Gospel of Mark or of John
   - Get a newer translation—a study Bible, if possible.
   - Each book in the Bible is divided into chapters and verses.

3. **Learning to Pray**
   - Just asking God only for things for yourself is selfish.
   - A balanced prayer approach follows the acronym ACTS:
     o Adoration
     o Confession
     o Thanksgiving
     o Supplication

4. **Set Aside a "Quiet Time"**
   - Spend 5 to 10 minutes every day with God.
   - Spend time reading the Bible, praying, and listening to God. A "quiet time" produces spiritual growth.
   - Ask God for guidance at the beginning of each day.

# 3. Temptations—Getting Victory over Sin

Before you made a commitment to Christ, you probably weren't as aware of sin as you are now. But now that you have begun your journey with Christ, the light of his gospel is probably making you aware of the darkness of sin. Let's explore the nature of sin, and then look at some strategies God has given us to get the upper hand.

## What Is Sin?

First, we need to understand about sin. Sin goes farther than individual sins—lying, cheating, adultery, murder. Sin springs from an attitude deep within us, an active or passive rebellion against God that places us and our desires first—a kind of inner selfish nature. Because of this root problem, our sinful actions sometimes surprise us.

## Sinful Nature

The Bible traces this kind of bent to selfishness and sinning in our human nature all the way back to Adam and Eve, the first human beings, who sinned against God.

But no matter what the cause is, you and I are stuck with the problem: a kind of inner rebellion that shows itself in moral weaknesses and sins of various kinds. On our own, even the best of us don't succeed in being completely sinless. As we saw in Lesson 1, that is why Jesus had to come to die for our sins, forgive us, and cleanse us.

## We Have an Adversary

But a sinful nature is not the only factor. We also have a spiritual adversary, an opponent. The Bible calls him Satan or the devil. In our world it is considered okay to believe in heaven and even angels. But if you believe in an actual Satan or the existence of hell, people scoff.

Jesus did not scoff. As you study his teachings, you find that he said more about Satan than anyone else in the Bible.

You are not the only person who has struggles with temptation. So did Jesus. Before he began his earthly ministry, Jesus went on a long retreat into the mountains to pray and prepare himself. There, Satan tempted him three times, attacking him at the point of his physical needs, his pride, and his calling to serve God (Luke 4:1-13).

Satan and his demons—the Bible reveals them as fallen angels (Luke 10:18; Revelation 12:9)—are your opponents and seek to tempt you and neutralize your influence. It's not like, "The devil made you do it." Demons don't have the power to grab you away from God (John 10:28), but they do try to deceive you and turn you to the wrong path.

## The Holy Spirit's Power Is Greater

Fortunately for us, God has not left us powerless against Satan. When we put our faith in Jesus as our Savior and Lord, something miraculous happens. The Holy Spirit, Christ's Spirit, comes to live within us. Jesus said:

> "Flesh gives birth to flesh, but the Spirit gives birth to spirit. You should not be surprised at my saying, 'You must be born again.'" (John 3:6-7)

Before we were Christians, we were merely human. But the new birth that Jesus talks about is the Holy Spirit making us alive spiritually.

> "Therefore, if anyone is in Christ, he is a new creation; the old has gone, the new has come!" (2 Corinthians 5:17)

> "No one who is born of God will continue to sin, because God's seed remains in him; he cannot go on sinning, because he has been born of God." (1 John 3:9)

Because God's Spirit is now living within us, sin is confronted, and we are given power to overcome it.

## What Can We Do to Stop Sinning?

You are probably finding that sins aren't very glamorous. Rather they are demoralizing and degrading. How can you escape them? Let me outline a series of strategies that will help you, though I'm not listing them in any particular order.

### Strategy 1. Trust in God

First of all, you must realize that God is with you to help you! He will never leave you. He is your Strength. He is your Help. The Bible reminds us:

> "You, dear children, are from God and have overcome them, because the one who is in you is greater than the one who is in the world." (1 John 4:4)

You are on the winning side. You have aligned yourself with Christ, who was victorious over sin and even death. Trust in him to help you.

### Strategy 2. Be Humble

Second, be humble. As long as you are proud and think you can fight sins in your own strength, you will fail. When you think that you are so strong that sin cannot touch you, you set yourself up for a fall. We are strong only in the Lord, not in ourselves.

## Strategy 3. Resist

Third, resist the temptation. God is building your character. Every time you say "No" to a temptation, it will be that much easier to say "No" the next time you are tempted. You are developing a healthy habit of saying "No" to temptation and "Yes" to God. Resist!

> "Submit yourselves, then, to God. Resist the devil, and he will flee from you." (James 4:7)

Don't flirt with a sin, trying to enjoy it without getting hurt by it. That is stupid. Resist the temptation and move on.

## Strategy 4. Flee

The fourth strategy may seem almost contradictory to the third. Flee!

> "Flee from sexual immorality." (1 Corinthians 6:18)

> "Flee the evil desires of youth...." (2 Timothy 2:22)

How can you resist when you are fleeing, running away?

There is a time to stand your ground and resist temptation. There is also a time to get as far away as you can from sources of temptation and, if possible, from the people who try to lead you astray.

If you struggle with lust, for example, stay away from situations and pornography that enflame your lust. If you struggle with alcohol abuse or drug addiction, stay away from situations where you will be tempted and from people who are indulging in these vices. When you identify "triggers" or strong temptations that tend to lead you into sin, carefully avoid them.

## Strategy 5. Embrace Truth

We human beings do what we believe in our heart of hearts to be true. If we *really* believe that true happiness lies in accumulating money, then we will be tempted to cheat, to steal, even to bend the truth to get money. If we *really* believe the ultimate source of happiness is having another human being love us or desire us sexually, then we find ourselves attracted to the wrong man or woman, and are subject to all kinds of compromise and weakness. The truths we hold most dear guide our lives.

When we make Jesus Christ our ultimate authority and begin to follow his teachings, the beliefs that previously motivated us are exposed as falsehoods. Jesus said:

> "If you hold to my teaching, you are really my disciples. Then you will know the truth, and the truth will set you free." (John 8:31-32)

This is why Scripture reading is so important. Gradually, we begin to align each aspect of our lives with truth, which weakens the temptation.

Scripture is helpful in times of temptation. When Jesus was tempted by Satan, he quoted Scripture to resist the temptation, saying: "It is written..." (Luke 4:1-13).

In Lesson 2 we talked about the importance of having a quiet time each day when you read the Bible and pray. I also encourage you to use this time to memorize the memory verse for each lesson. This will help you to internalize the truth contained in the verse so it will strengthen you. The Psalmist said:

> "I have hidden your word in my heart that I might not sin against you." (Psalms 119:11)

## Strategy 6. Pray

Of course, prayer is of great help in temptation, since it connects us directly with God by faith. In the Lord's Prayer, Jesus teaches his disciples to pray for help when we are weak: "Lead us not into temptation, but deliver us from evil" (or "from the evil one", Matthew 6:13). In the Garden of Gethsemane before his crucifixion, Jesus resisted temptation by means of prayer. He told the disciples who were nearby:

> "Watch and pray so that you will not fall into temptation. The spirit is willing, but the body is weak." (Matthew 26:41)

Prayer strengthens us, so we must "watch" (that is, stay awake and alert) and pray. When we focus on the sin and the temptation, *sin* has our attention. When we turn to God in prayer then *God* has our focus and attention, weakening the temptation.

## Strategy 7. Love God and Embrace His Love for You

The seventh strategy is to embrace God's love. When you believe that God loves you greatly, sin becomes the disappointing of the one you love, rather than the breaking of some impersonal rule or law. Love is the unique glory of Christianity. God loves you, even though you have sinned. Love is more powerful than temptation.

# What If You *Do* Fall to Temptation?

But what if you *do* sin? What if you fall to temptation? The Apostle John wrote:

> "My dear children, I write this to you so that you will not sin. But if anybody does sin, we have one who speaks to the Father in our defense—Jesus Christ, the Righteous One. He is the atoning sacrifice for our sins, and not only for ours but also for the sins of the whole world." (1 John 2:1-2)

Even when we sin after becoming Christians, there is forgiveness for us. Thank God! Jesus is the atoning sacrifice for all my sins and yours—past, present, and future.

# Repentance, Confession, and Forgiveness

Here is what to do. The Apostle John tells us:

> "If we confess our sins, he is faithful and just and will forgive us our sins and purify us from all unrighteousness." (1 John 1:9)

I can't begin to tell you how much this promise has meant to me. I memorized it as a young Christian and have said it over and over again when I became aware that I had sinned. You should memorize it, too.

Let me explain three concepts:

**1. Repentance** is sorrow for your sin and the willingness to turn away from it. This is not sorrow for getting "caught," but sorrow that you have disappointed the Father you love.

**2. Confession**, which follows repentance, is telling God (or another Christian) that you have sinned. This is not simplistic. There is great power in saying directly and aloud (1) that you have sinned and (2) the exact nature of your sin—without making any excuse.

Confession moves what was done in the darkness into the light where it can be healed.

> "But if we walk in the light, as he is in the light, we have fellowship with one another, and the blood of Jesus, his Son, purifies us from all sin." (1 John 1:7)

Many Christians have discovered the value of having a close Christian friend or accountability partner with whom they can be honest and to whom they can confess their sins (James 5:16). Confession is a declaration of truth and therefore powerful. Confession helps restore and strengthen you.

**3. Receiving Forgiveness.** Third, you must receive forgiveness. Believe that God does indeed forgive you! Remember:

> "If we confess our sins, he is faithful and just and will **forgive** us our sins and **purify** us from all unrighteousness." (1 John 1:9)

This promise has two parts: (1) **forgiveness**—that God will forgive us our sins and not hold them against us any longer, and (2) **cleansing**—that God will purify us or cleanse us from our sins, so we don't have to feel dirty any longer. We are washed! (1 Corinthians 6:9-11). We are clean before God again.

Sometimes you may still *feel* dirty and degraded. That is Satan trying to trick you and drag you down. Resist it and take hold of God's promise for you that he "will forgive us and purify us." God forgives you!

## Temptation Is Not Sin

Realize that temptation is not the same as sin. Sometimes being tempted makes us *feel* dirty, but temptation is not sin. Jesus was severely tempted, but that does not mean he was contaminated with the sin. When asked about temptation, Reformation leader Martin Luther is reputed to have said:

> "You can't help it if a bird flies over your head,
> but you can stop it from building a nest in your hair."

## There Is No End to God's Forgiveness

When I was younger in the faith, I used to despair when I found myself committing the same sin time after time. I'm not worthy to be forgiven, I'd tell myself. (Which is true.) God will give up on me. (Which is *not* true!)

One on occasion, St. Peter came to Jesus in extreme frustration.

> "'Lord, how many times shall I forgive my brother when he sins against me? Up to seven times?'
> Jesus answered, 'I tell you, not seven times, but seventy-seven times.'" (Matthew 18:21-22)

God has no limit to the number of times he will forgive your sins.

## Is It Worth the Struggle?

It really *is* worth the struggle. As we walk with Jesus on this journey, we will experience the joy of his presence, the health and rightness of his Way, and the blessings that come through walking with God himself.

As you walk with the Lord, you *will* become stronger. Gradually, you will be able to resist temptation to sins that used to overpower you. Don't give up! Jesus tells his disciples:

> "I have told you these things, so that in me you may have peace. In this world you will have trouble. But take heart! I have overcome the world." (John 16:33)

### Prayer

Lord, sometimes temptation seems so strong. Thank you for teaching us how to resist temptation and more and more be free from sin so we can walk with you in joy. Forgive us where we have failed you. We know you do—and that is what keeps us going. Thank you for your love for us. Thank you that you believe in us—in spite of ourselves. In your name, Jesus, we pray. Amen.

## Participant Guide. 3. Temptations—Getting Victory over Sin

### Memory Verse

"If we confess our sins, he is faithful and just and will forgive us our sins and purify us from all unrighteousness." (1 John 1:9, NIV)

### Questions and Discussion Points

1. **Read aloud** five times your new memory verse (1 John 1:9) and copy it onto a card.
2. **Report** how your daily quiet time is going. Discuss any problems you are having with setting aside the time, interruptions, tiredness, etc.
3. **Baptism.** Have you made an appointment yet to discuss baptism with a pastor? If so, what is the process in your church for being baptized?
4. **Discuss.** What is sin? In what way is it part of our fallen human nature?
5. **Discuss.** Does Satan make us sin? If not, what part does he have in temptation?
6. **Discuss.** How does the Holy Spirit help us resist sin?
7. **Discuss.** What strategies can help us resist temptation? Which of these strategies seem to work best for you?
8. **Discuss.** What is the difference between repentance and confession? How does confession strengthen you to resist temptation the next time you are tempted?
9. **Discuss.** How do you know that God will forgive you when you sin again and again? Is there a point where he stops forgiving you?
10. **Discuss.** When you are tempted, is that a sin, even though you are able to resist the temptation?
11. **Review** the memory verses for Lesson 1 (Ephesians 2:8-9) and Lesson 2 (John 8:31-32). Keep working on your memory verses during the week so you are able to say them without any mistakes. By the way, when you say the verse, also say the reference after the verse. Why don't you challenge your mentor that you can say the verses better than he or she next week.
12. **Pray.** Discuss with your mentor which sins you are having the most trouble resisting. Then pray with your mentor, asking God for help to resist temptation and for forgiveness.
13. **Appointment.** Set a time and place to meet and go through next week's lesson.

### Outline of Lesson 3. Temptations — Getting Victory over Sin

1. **Basics about sin**
   - Sin springs from a deep active or passive rebellion against God, resulting in sinful actions.
   - We humans have a sinful nature, traced back to Adam and Eve.
   - We have an adversary, Satan or the devil.
     - He is an actual spiritual person.

- o   Jesus taught about him.
- o   Jesus was tempted by Satan prior to his ministry.
- o   Demons, fallen angels who serve Satan, also seek to tempt us.
- The Holy Spirit's power is greater than Satan's power.
  - o   The Holy Spirit gives us spiritual life. We are "born again" by the Spirit (John 3:6-7).
  - o   The Holy Spirit makes us alive spiritually (2 Corinthians 5:17).
  - o   The Holy Spirit gives us power over the tyranny of sin (1 John 3:9).

2.  **Strategies that help us stop sinning**
    - Trust in God. God is with you to help you in this battle (1 John 4:4).
    - Be Humble. You can't win this battle by yourself, only when you find your strength in God.
    - Resist the temptation. Don't flirt with a sin, but resist it firmly (James 4:7)
    - Flee from sin's temptation (1 Corinthians 6:18; 2 Timothy 2:22). Stay away from people and situations that tend to lead you into sin.
    - Embrace truth.
      - o   We do what we really believe to be true.
      - o   When we embrace the truth taught by Jesus, we will stop believing the false beliefs that lead us into sin (John 8:31-32).
      - o   Scripture memory is a way of embracing and internalizing truth (Psalms 119:11).
    - Pray when you are tempted.
      - o   The Lord's Prayer teaches us to pray about temptation (Matthew 6:13).
      - o   Jesus prayed when he was tempted.
      - o   Jesus taught his disciples to pray when they were tempted (Matthew 26:41).
    - Love God and embrace his love for you.
      - o   When you see sin as an offence against one you love, it is easier to resist.

3.  **What If You *Do* Fall to Temptation?**
    - o   Christians do sin after their conversion, but there is forgiveness for us.
    - o   Jesus is the atoning sacrifice for our sins (1 John 2:1-2).
    - Repentance is sorrow for sin and willingness to turn away from it.
    - Confession is stating that you have sinned—no excuses. Confession moves us from darkness to light (1 John 1:7).
    - Receiving forgiveness. God promises to (1) forgive you and (2) cleanse you from your sin (1 John 1:9). Temptation is not sin
    - There is no end to God's forgiveness (Matthew 18:21-22; John 16:33)

# 4. Fellowship—Connecting to a Community of Christians

Some people try to live a Christian life by themselves, away from any regular Christian friends or a church. It does not work very well–either for their own growth or to accomplish Jesus' mission here on earth.

## Love Can't Operate in a Vacuum

The reason we can't practice authentic Christianity without Christian fellowship is because love is at the very root of God's character.

"God is love. Whoever lives in love lives in God, and God in him." (1 John 4:16)

Love requires someone to love. Love seeks out someone to love and bless. Love is never solitary. It requires community to operate. Jesus believed in this so much that he made this audacious statement:

"A new command I give you: Love one another. As I have loved you, so you must love one another. By this all men will know that you are my disciples, if you love one another." (John 13:34-35)

We start out selfish on our own, but when we are with others, we learn to care for their needs. Have you ever seen how a young man settles down when he gets married? Have you ever seen a young woman begin to mature when she becomes a mother? Why does this happen? Because marriage and family require people to put others' needs first. They require people to learn to love.

The Bible describes communities of Christians in four ways: as a family, as a body, as a flock, and as a church.

## 1. We Are Part of a Family

First, let's look at the idea of Christians as a family. Look at these verses:

"Let us do good to all people, especially to those who belong to the **family of believers**." (Galatians 6:10)

"Finally, all of you, live in harmony with one another; be sympathetic, **love as brothers**, be compassionate and humble." (1 Peter 3:8)

Family members care for each other, help each other, support each other—and forgive each other when they have an argument. We are family, sons and daughters of the same Father.

## 2. We Are Part of a Body

Christians are also described as part of a body.

> "The **body is a unit**, though it is made up of **many parts**; and though all its parts are many, they form **one body**. So it is with Christ." (1 Corinthians 12:12)

> "From him the whole body, joined and held together by every supporting ligament, grows and builds itself up in love, as **each part does its work**." (Ephesians 4:16)

Parts of a body aren't independent, but interdependent. Each part has a vital responsibility—as a finger, or an eye, or a knee, for example—to help the whole body function well. A toe can't isolate itself from the body and survive.

## 3. We Are Part of a Flock

Christians are also described as part of a flock under the care of a shepherd. The shepherd is not passive. Rather, he is active in finding food for the flock, taking them to streams where they can drink, binding up the wounds of those who are injured, and protecting the flock against predators. Sometimes the shepherd must defend the sheep at the risk of his life. Jesus said:

> "I am the good shepherd. The good shepherd lays down his life for the sheep." (John 10:11)

This idea of a shepherd is carried over to the church that Jesus founded. The word "pastor" literally means "shepherd." Each grouping of Christians has a pastor or shepherd who is responsible for the "flock" or that grouping of Christ-followers. The Apostle Paul exhorted some leaders:

> "Keep watch over yourselves and all the **flock** of which the Holy Spirit has made you overseers. Be **shepherds** of the church of God, which he bought with his own blood." (Acts 20:28)

Sometimes these Christian leaders are called elders, priests, ministers, bishops, or overseers. Do not let the terminology confuse you. Just understand the concept of shepherds caring for the sheep—God's people.

## 4. We Are Part of the Church

The "church" is very much Jesus' idea—but Jesus' concept of church may be quite a bit different than many "churches" that you may see around you. Let me clarify.

Jesus said: "I will build my church" (Matthew 16:18). The Bible word "church" means, literally, "the called-out ones," those who have been called by God and gathered together out of the world.

Notice carefully that the word "church" does *not* mean a building! A church is primarily a gathering of people, not a physical structure. In fact, for the first few centuries after Christ, there were no church buildings. People met for worship in homes.

Since the primary concept of the church is people, you don't "go to church." Rather you gather with the church. In fact, it is extremely important for you to gather regularly with a church, a congregation, or group of Christians near you. It is vital for your health and growth. The Bible says:

> "**Let us not give up meeting together**, as some are in the habit of doing, but let us **encourage one another**—and all the more as you see the Day approaching." (Hebrews 10:25)

## Large, Small, and Pairs

Let's look at the value of various groupings of God's people:

- **Larger gatherings**. In our day, churches range in size from 25 to 5,000 and even more. Size has nothing to do with spiritual quality—bigger is not necessarily better. In larger gatherings you worship with other Christians and hear teaching and preaching that can help you grow in Christ.

- **Small groups**. Smaller gatherings are important for you also, because here you get to know your Christian brothers and sisters well. In small groups they can get to know you, love you, and care for you—and vice versa. This is where the best Christian fellowship takes place. These small groups are sometimes called by different names—"life groups," "care groups," etc. You need to be part of one of these. Ask your mentor or the pastor of your church how to get involved in a small group.

- **Pairs**. Another important way to grow is to spend time on a regular basis with one or two Christian friends. I hope that you are following my instructions and are doing this *Beginning the Journey* study with a mentor. If not, you need to find a person with whom you can study. Having a close Christian friend gives you someone to be accountable to—in a good way. Accountability keeps you on track and growing.

## How Do You Find a Church?

The best way to find a church is to ask your mentor or Christian friend what church he or she attends and go along. Going with a friend makes it easier to get acquainted with other Christians and learn about Christian worship and life in a church.

Sometimes, however, finding the right church for you can be difficult. For one reason or another, a church may not "feel right" to you. If that is the case, try attending another church in your community, if one is available.

But no church is perfect. That is because churches are made up of human beings (just like you). Whatever church you attend, you will probably see some flaws. Do not focus on the flaws. Focus on God—how you can worship him in that service and what you can learn from him through the preaching or teaching.

## What to Look For

Churches come in all shapes and sizes. There are different denominations or families of churches that come from different historical traditions. Do not chose a church by its name. Instead, look for a church:

- **That teaches or preaches from the Bible.** Avoid churches where the sermon or message is mainly the preacher's own thoughts and theories. You will grow from Bible teaching, not just clever sermons.
- **Where people love one another.** Remember, Jesus said that love is the sign that they are his true disciples (John 13:34-35).
- **That is not proud and exclusive.** Some offshoots of Christianity, called sects, act as if all other churches are wrong and only they have the truth. Avoid these churches. They have some truth, but their exclusive attitude leads to serious problems and distortions of Jesus' teachings.

## Benefits of Being Part of a Church

There are many benefits and blessings of being part of a church. Jesus intended it this way.

- **Role models.** You can find people who are mature in the Christian faith from whom you can learn and who you can model your life after. These are like fathers and mothers for us in the faith.

- **Specialized ministries.** In a church you will find people who have received special spiritual gifts from God that will help build you up in the faith. You will meet people with gifts of teaching, evangelism, faith, showing mercy, exhortation, encouragement, prayer, artistic gifts such as music and art, and many others. A church is designed to offer a rich environment of spiritually gifted people who together produce a healthy Christian community.

- **Protection.** A church provides spiritual protection for you. The role of a pastor or shepherd is to watch out for you and other members of the flock (Galatians 6:1).

- **Healing.** A church is designed to be a place where hurting, wounded people can find love and healing. The love that produces healing flows best in smaller groups, so be sure to become part of such a group.

- **Encouragement.** Face it. Sometimes we get discouraged. Having brothers and sisters nearby can help us. The Bible says, "Encourage one another and build each other up" (1 Thessalonians 5:11). "Carry each other's burdens, and in this way you will fulfill the law of Christ" (Galatians 6:2).

- **Growth.** If you are part of a healthy church, you will find yourself growing and becoming more mature in your faith.

## You Have a Lot to Offer, Too

Perhaps you have been thinking about what you can *receive* from a church. That is good. But also realize that you have a lot to *offer* a Christian community. Just like having a baby energizes a human family, so having new Christians energizes a church. People praise God for what Jesus has done in your life.

God has given you spiritual gifts to help others in the Christian community. Though you may not realize yet what these gifts are, your presence and faithfulness will help build up the church and make everyone else stronger.

## Be Faithful

As we have learned, Jesus started the Christian faith on the principle of a loving community of disciples. To be his followers, we need to become a part of a community of believers. That is our responsibility. I have two recommendations:

1. **Become part of a small group**. Being in a group of 6 to 12 people every week or two will help you a great deal. It is well worth your time!
2. **Join a church in your community**. Church membership may seem a little scary, but don't quit. Becoming a formal member of a church is an important step for your spiritual growth. It usually involves some classes and baptism. Just like marriage signals commitment and causes growth and fulfillment, so joining a church signals commitment and produces growth and fulfillment.

## Don't Be a "Church-Hopper"

You will find some people who are "church-hoppers." Like grasshoppers or crickets, they jump from church to church, never staying long, but hopping to another church. They look for perfection, but never find it. So they hop off again. These immature people are afflicted with three problems:

1. **Selfishness**. They are more concerned with what they can *get*, than what they can *give*. People who hop from one church to another never stay long enough to use their spiritual gifts to build others up. Selfishness is the opposite of love.
2. **Lack of realism**. They expect churches to be perfect, and when they find a church's flaws, they're gone. They're like dreamy-eyed young married couples who expect marriage to be perfect. Hopefully, they grow up and begin to work at making the best of their relationship.
3. **Unfaithfulness**. They lack commitment or faithfulness. One of the qualities Jesus seeks to produce in his followers is faithfulness or reliability—steadfastness. Commitment causes growth in us and health in a church body.

When Jesus founded the Christian faith, he founded it on love—love for God and love for one another. He knew that Christian fellowship was the network through which this love would flow. That is why it is important to become part of a Christian fellowship ourselves.

## Prayer

Lord, thank you for the people who have followed Jesus before me. I have learned so much from them. I pray that you will help each person studying this lesson to find a place where he or she can be part of a fellowship of Christian brothers and sisters. Guide them, help them, so that they can grow strong in Jesus. In his name, I pray. Amen.

## Participant Guide: 4. Fellowship—Connecting to a Community

### Memory Verse

"A new command I give you: Love one another. As I have loved you, so you must love one another. By this all men will know that you are my disciples, if you love one another." (John 13:34-35, NIV)

### Questions and Discussion Points

1. **Read aloud** five times the new memory verse (John 13:34-35) and copy it onto a card.
2. **Discuss.** Why does God's nature of love require that Jesus' followers be part of a community?
3. **Discuss.** What are four communities that Christian gatherings are compared to in the Bible?

   _____ (Hint: A group consisting of blood relatives.)
   _____ (Hint: The flesh and blood part of you.)
   _____ (Hint: A group of wooly animals.)
   _____ (Hint: The word literally means "the called-out-ones")

   What unique truths about the church does each of these analogies teach us?
4. **Discuss.** What benefits do you receive by being part of a church?
5. **Discuss.** Why are small groups important for your spiritual growth?
6. **Discuss.** What is wrong with "church hopping," going from one church to another without settling down?
7. **Discuss.** Why aren't any churches perfect? If this is so, according to John 13:34-35, why is loving one another a true sign of being authentic disciples of Jesus?
8. **Attend church with your mentor**, if you haven't already done so. Discuss what impressions you had of the people in this church.
9. **What kinds of responsibilities** has your mentor had in a church or small group? How has a church or small group helped your mentor?
10. **Baptism.** Have you arranged to be baptized yet? If not, what is keeping you from moving forward with this?
11. **Discuss.** Last lesson we talked about resisting temptation. How is that going?
12. **Assignment for mentor**: Introduce your new Christian friend to several of your believer friends. You are the bridge for your Christian friend to the Christian community.
13. **Assignment for new Christian:** Have coffee or a meal with some of your mentor's friends from his or her church or small group. If you go to a restaurant or coffee shop, ask your mentor to pay the bill. ☺
14. **Review your memory verses** from Lesson 1 (Ephesians 2:8-9), Lesson 2 (John 8:31-32), and Lesson 3 (1 John 1:9). Can you say them more accurately than your mentor can? (Hey, mentor! You need to learn these, too.)

15. **Pray together** about you finding a regular church or small group to help you grow strong as Jesus' disciple. Also pray about any problems that you are experiencing.

16. **Ask your mentor** if he or she has any problems that you can pray for. If you feel comfortable, pray for your mentor's need right now. Praying for each other is one way we show our love for each other.

17. **Appointment**. Set a time and place to meet and go through next week's lesson.


## Outline of Lesson 4. Connecting to a Community of Christians

1. **The Christian community is where we learn to love**
   - Love is the root of God's character (1 John 4:16).
   - Love requires someone to love, it is not solitary.
   - Jesus said love is our distinguishing characteristic (John 13:34-35).
   - Love leads us into maturity.

2. **The Bible describes the church in four ways. We are part of a:**
   - Family (Galatians 6:10; 1 Peter 3:8), sons and daughters of the same Father.
   - Body (1 Corinthians 12:12; Ephesians 4:16), we are interdependent, like different parts of a human body.
   - Flock, cared for and protected by a shepherd (John 10:11). Human shepherds are called elders, priests, ministers, bishops, or overseers (Acts 20:28).
   - Church (Matthew 16:18), a society of "the called-out ones."
     o The word "church" refers to the people, not to a building.
     o Gathering regularly is to help us grow (Hebrews 10:25).

3. **Types of Christian Groupings**
   - Larger gatherings are for worship together and teaching.
   - Small groups are where we connect for love and caring for each other and experience.
   - Christian fellowship.
   - Pairs, a mentor with a newer Christian helps you grow, too.

4. **How to Find a Church**
   - No church is perfect. You are there to focus on God, not the flaws.
   - Look for a church:
     o That teaches or preaches from the Bible.
     o Where people love one another.
     o That is not proud and exclusive.

5. **Benefits of being part of a church**
   - Role models
   - Specialized ministries and spiritual gifts
   - Protection
   - Healing
   - Encouragement
   - Growth

   You have a lot to offer a church also.

6. **Be faithful** as (1) part of a small group and (2) a church. Then stay put.
   Don't be a "church hopper" who is: Selfish, Unrealistic, and Unfaithful.

# 5. Love—the Core of Christianity

If you were to believe some people, they would say that Christianity is based on guilt and fear. They are wrong.

World religions conceive of God in various ways—Creator, just Judge, Merciful One, impersonal Force, Essence of Truth, Ultimate Reality, Omnipotent One, and the list goes on.

But the Christian faith is unique in understanding God as love—and the implications of this are profound!

## God Is Love

When you peel the God of Christianity down to his very core, you find love. Consider this Bible passage (which is your memory verse for this lesson):

"Dear friends, let us love one another, for love comes from God. Everyone who loves has been born of God and knows God. Whoever does not love does not know God, because God is love." (1 John 4:7-8)

What does "God is love" mean? Yes, the Bible teaches that God is just and omnipotent and merciful. But the trademark characteristic of God is love. God is love.

## God Is the First Lover

God is the source and inspiration for our own love.

"We love because he first loved us." (1 John 4:19)

Any kind of love that we experience for friends, for family, for that someone special—all of it had its root in God, since the Bible teaches that we are made in God's image (Genesis 1:27). We are designed according to his own "template."

## God Loves Us

Perhaps the most wonderful and profound truth that you can grasp is that the God of the universe knows you individually and loves you personally and abundantly. The most famous verse in the New Testament spells this out:

"For God so loved the world that he gave his one and only Son, that whoever believes in him shall not perish but have eternal life." (John 3:16)

Jesus' prime motivation to come to our world was love.

## God Loves Us in Spite of Ourselves

A second truth is this: God loves us in spite of ourselves. It is very common to think that because of your sins, God does not love you anymore. That may be the way *you feel* about yourself, but it does not describe *God's feelings* toward you. Consider:

"But God demonstrates his own love for us in this: **While we were still sinners**, Christ died for us." (Romans 5:8)

"But because of his great love for us, God, who is rich in mercy, made us alive with Christ **even when we were dead in transgressions**—it is by grace you have been saved." (Ephesians 2:4-5)

And another verse that we have seen already:

"For it is **by grace** you have been saved, through faith—and this **not from yourselves**, it is the gift of God—not by works, so that no one can boast." (Ephesians 2:8-9)

God does not love us because we are good and worth loving. No, he loved us when we were still rebellious against him, when we were sinning, when we were despicable.

## The Two Greatest Commandments

If the essence of God's nature is love, then it follows that he desires his children to love. When Jesus was asked what were the most important commands in the Bible—out of the hundreds of instructions in the Old Testament—Jesus singled out two:

"'Love the Lord your God with all your heart and with all your soul and with all your mind.'[1] This is the first and greatest commandment. And the second is like it: 'Love your neighbor as yourself.'"[2] (Matthew 22:37-39)

Let us look at these more closely:

### 1. Love God

First, we are commanded to love God supremely—with all our heart, soul, and mind. How do you learn to love God? Through prayer and worship. By walking through your life conscious of him and seeking to please him. To love God means that we seek to obey him. Loving God is first—not down the ladder of priorities that guide our lives, but top rung!

### 2. Love Our Neighbor

Second, we are commanded to love our neighbor. Who qualifies as "neighbor"? Someone asked Jesus that. In response he told the story of the Good Samaritan, where a Samaritan man (a person from a hated ethnic and religious minority) showed mercy towards an injured Jew (his natural enemy). In other words, even our enemies are to be subjects of our love; they are our neighbors (Luke 10:29-37).

[1] Quoting Deuteronomy 6:5.
[2] Quoting Leviticus 19:18.

## We Will Experience Persecution

As you may have learned already, being a committed Christian exposes you to persecution. In some regions, the persecution is mild, but in some places persecution of Christians includes threat of physical violence. St. Paul wrote to his protégé Timothy:

> "In fact, everyone who wants to live a godly life in Christ Jesus will be persecuted." (2 Timothy 3:12)

Persecution has a way of sorting out the true disciples from those who are only enthusiastic temporarily. Jesus taught in the Parable of the Sower:

> "The one who received the seed that fell on rocky places is the man who hears the word and at once receives it with joy. But since he has no root, he lasts only a short time. When trouble or persecution comes because of the word, he quickly falls away." (Matthew 13:20-21)

## We Are to Love Our Enemies

Nevertheless, Jesus' teaching is clear:

> "I tell you: Love your enemies and pray for those who persecute you." (Matthew 5:44)

Dear friends, this is radical! No other religion teaches that we should love our enemies! But because the core of God is love, this love extends even to God's enemies (as we once were), and must extend to our enemies, too. We are instructed:

> "Bless those who persecute you; bless and don't curse." (Romans 12:14)

You see, love is the guiding principle, the engine that drives Christian living.

## Love Causes Us to Forgive Those Who Sin Against Us

Jesus' first word from the cross reflected this radical love:

> "Father, forgive them, for they don't know what they are doing." (Luke 23:34a)

The will to forgive flows from this love at the core of God. Forgiveness is expected of Jesus' followers, too. At the center of the Lord's Prayer we find this request:

> "Forgive us our debts,
> as we also have forgiven our debtors." (Matthew 6:12)

"Debts," of course, represent sins. We are praying that God will forgive our sins *in the same way* as we forgive those who have sinned against us. In the measure that we forgive, we will be forgiven. And in case his disciples did not quite get the point, Jesus stated it more clearly yet:

> "For if you forgive men when they sin against you, your heavenly Father will also forgive you. But if you don't forgive men their sins, your Father will not forgive your sins." (Matthew 6:14-15)

This is a hard saying. Jesus says that if we want to be recipients of God's love and for-giveness, that we must let it flow on through us to others. We cannot receive forgiveness without giving it as well.

There are people who have hurt you—sometimes deeply! Usually it is the people who are closest to us who are able to hurt us the most. Have you forgiven these people who have sinned deeply against you? Jesus asks you to do that.

To forgive does not mean that you now trust them and are suddenly close friends again. Nor does it excuse what they have done or minimize the hurt and destruction they have caused. But it means that you have decided in your heart to no longer hold their sin against them—ever again. Sometimes we don't think we are able to do this—the hurt is so fresh and the wound so tender. But pray and ask God to help you forgive, and he will.

As you have probably guessed by now, this love teaching is not just pretty and nice, it is difficult and costly. Think what it cost Jesus to die on the cross for your sin. It was not a cheap forgiveness. It cost him. Neither will it be easy and trivial for you to forgive, but God calls you to this. That is what it means to love.

## Love Is Not a Sign of Weakness, but of Strength

Sometimes hard, street-wise people think that love is a sign of weakness. It is a jungle out there—kill or be killed. There is no place for forgiveness. If you are weak, you die.

Frankly, that is a pretty shallow, naïve view of love. Love is the strongest force in the world—stronger than armies and dictators, stronger than evil, stronger than pain. When you look at Jesus' voluntary death on the cross, you don't see weakness, but strength. You see determination to love in the face of evil and hate. The Apostle Paul tells us:

> "'If your enemy is hungry, feed him; if he is thirsty, give him something to drink....'[3] Do not be overcome by evil, but overcome evil with good." (Romans 12:20-21)

In the mid-twentieth century, African-Americans, especially in the American South, were discriminated against and treated as second-class citizens. And all this was supported by laws.

Dr. Martin Luther King, Jr., led a non-violent, prayer-based movement to obtain civil rights. He was jailed many times, but persisted in praying for his persecutors and led his followers to pray for and to have love for those who opposed them. Contrast that to the race riots that flared up in cities after he was no longer there to lead. The civil rights laws in place today are a result of love, not hate, of prayer, not violence. Love is strong.

## The Golden Rule

One practical way of assessing our love is by the so-called Golden Rule. It helps us separate our own selfish tendencies from the loving thing to do. Jesus taught us:

---

[3] Quotation from Proverbs 25:21.

"So in everything, do to others what you would have them do to you, for this sums up the Law and the Prophets." (Matthew 7:12)

Just as the two greatest commandments sum up the teachings of the whole Bible ("the Law and the Prophets"), so does the Golden Rule. Treat other people the way you would like to be treated yourself.

## The Classic Statement of Love

We will conclude this lesson by reading the classic "love chapter" in the Bible, 1 Corinthians, chapter 13. I encourage you to read it out loud and then think deeply about it this week:

"If I speak in the tongues of men and of angels, but have not love, I am only a resounding gong or a clanging cymbal. If I have the gift of prophecy and can fathom all mysteries and all knowledge, and if I have a faith that can move mountains, but have not love, I am nothing. If I give all I possess to the poor and surrender my body to the flames, but have not love, I gain nothing.

"Love is patient, love is kind. It does not envy, it does not boast, it is not proud. It is not rude, it is not self-seeking, it is not easily angered, it keeps no record of wrongs. Love does not delight in evil but rejoices with the truth. It always protects, always trusts, always hopes, always perseveres.

"Love never fails. But where there are prophecies, they will cease; where there are tongues, they will be stilled; where there is knowledge, it will pass away. For we know in part and we prophesy in part, but when perfection comes, the imperfect disappears. When I was a child, I talked like a child, I thought like a child, I reasoned like a child. When I became a man, I put childish ways behind me. Now we see but a poor reflection as in a mirror; then we shall see face to face. Now I know in part; then I shall know fully, even as I am fully known.

"And now these three remain: faith, hope and love. But the greatest of these is love." (1 Corinthians 13:1-13)

### Prayer

Father, your love is deep and strong. You loved me and rescued me from the way I was going. I can begin to see how you want me to start loving with the same consistency and power that you love. Help me to forgive the people who have hurt me. Help me to love the people around me who don't deserve love. To be like you I need you to transform my natural inclinations and help me. But I trust you to do that. In Jesus' name, I pray. Amen.

## Participant Guide: 5. Love—the Core of Christianity

### Memory Verse

"Dear friends, let us love one another, for love comes from God. Everyone who loves has been born of God and knows God. Whoever does not love does not know God, because God is love." (1 John 4:7-8, NIV)

### Questions and Discussion Points

1. **Read aloud your memory verse** for this week (1 John 4:7-8). Write it on a card.
2. **Report.** Did you attend a church last week? What did you like about it? What didn't you like about it? What didn't you understand?
3. **Report.** How is your quiet time? Are you spending time regularly with God? What time of day is working best for you?
4. **Discuss.** Why is a God of love so radically different from the gods of this world?
5. **Discuss.** What happens to you when you finally understand that God loves you just the way you are?
6. **Discuss.** What are the two greatest commandments? How do we fulfill the first commandment? How do we fulfill the second commandment?
7. **Discuss.** Does it make any sense to love your enemies? Why should you love them? Is there a time when you were God's enemy? Is love a sign of weakness?
8. **Discuss.** Why is it so important that you forgive those who have hurt you?
9. **Discuss.** Does forgiving a person mean that you must trust him? Why or why not?
10. **Discuss.** Who are the people who have hurt you most? Why is it so hard to forgive them? Mentor: Share how some people have hurt you and how you came to forgive them.
11. **Assignment.** Make a list of the people who you have trouble forgiving. Then pray daily that God will help you forgive them.
12. **Review your memory verses** from Lesson 1 (Ephesians 2:8-9), Lesson 2 (John 8:31-32), Lesson 3 (1 John 1:9), and Lesson 4 (John 13:34-35). See if you can say them more accurately than your mentor can.
13. **Pray together** about the people you need to forgive. Include in your prayers any problems that you or your mentor are experiencing in your lives. If you haven't learned to pray aloud with your mentor, start today by praying a one-sentence prayer.
14. **Appointment.** Set a time and place to meet and go through next week's lesson.

## Outline of Lesson 5. Love—the Core of Christianity

1. **Jesus' view of love makes the Christian faith unique among all the world religions**
   - God is love (1 John 4:7-8). Love is his trademark and core quality.
   - God is the first lover who inspires our love (1 John 4:19), and he provides the template or image in which we were made (Genesis 1:27).
   - God loves us in spite of ourselves (John 3:16; Romans 5:8; Ephesians 2:4-5, 8-9). Even before we were Christians, God loved us.

2. **The Two Greatest Commandments (Matthew 22:37-39)**
   - Love God supremely.
   - Love our neighbor as ourselves, e.g. the Good Samaritan (Luke 10:29-37).

3. **The Implications of the Command to Love**
   - We will experience persecution (2 Timothy 3:12; Matthew 13:20-21), but we are to love our enemies, our persecutors (Matthew 5:44; Romans 12:14).
   - Love causes us to forgive those who sin against us.
     - o Jesus modeled forgiveness on the cross (Luke 23:34a).
     - o Forgiveness is taught in the Lord's Prayer (Matthew 6:12, 14-15).
     - o If we want to be forgiven, we must forgive those who sin against us.
     - o Forgiveness doesn't imply trust, or excuse of actions, or minimize the hurt.
     - o Forgiveness means you have decided not to hold their sin against them any longer.
     - o If this seems impossible, ask for God's help.
   - Love Is Not a Sign of Weakness, but of Strength.
     - o Love is the strongest force in the world.
     - o Love overcomes evil and hate (Romans 12:20-21).
     - o Example: Non-violent civil rights movement under Dr. Martin Luther King, Jr.

4. **Two Classic Statements of Love**
   - The Golden Rule (Matthew 7:12)
   - The "Love Chapter" (1 Corinthians 13)

# 6. Gospel—Understanding Christ's Story

The word "gospel" occurs 98 times in the New Testament, but if you were to ask the average man or woman, he or she probably would not be able to define it.

"Gospel" in the Bible actually means "good news."

So what is this Good News about Jesus? If you listened to some angry preachers, you would think that the gospel is that you are a sinner and condemned to hell without Jesus. While that may be true, that is bad news, not good news! So what is the good news?

Let's examine some of the elements of the Good News or the Gospel.

## 1. God Loves Us

The first piece of amazing Good News is that God loves us. He is not in an angry rage. Yes, our sins separated us from him, but he loves us! He is willing to go to the limit to rescue and help us. He isn't so preoccupied with running multiple galaxies that he can't be bothered. He loves us. If anything is good news, this is! In Lesson 5 we spent considerable time examining God's love for us.

## 2. Jesus Is God in the Flesh

The second piece of amazing Good News is that Jesus is not just a great teacher and honored prophet. He is God in the flesh, a truth called "the incarnation."[1] The Jews considered this blasphemous. Even today, some people shy away from it. But the Bible is clear: Jesus is the divine Son of God.

It started when Jesus was conceived in a virgin—not by a human husband, but by the Holy Spirit. The angel said to Mary:

> "The Holy Spirit will come upon you, and the power of the Most High will overshadow you. So the holy one to be born will be called the Son of God." (Luke 1:35)

---

[1] You can learn more about this in my online Bible study, "Christmas Incarnation" (www.jesuswalk.com/christmas-incarnation/), also available as a book.

Jesus was born into a poor and humble family, so poor that Jesus' first cradle was a cattle manger. But the night he was born, an angel choir announced his birth:

> "Today in the town of David a Savior has been born to you; he is Christ the Lord." (Luke 2:11)

Though Jesus did not proclaim publically that he was the Messiah or Christ until the end of his ministry, during his trial this interchange took place:

> "The high priest said to him, 'I charge you under oath by the living God: Tell us if you are the Christ, the Son of God.'
>
> 'Yes, it is as you say,' Jesus replied. 'But I say to all of you: In the future you will see the Son of Man sitting at the right hand of the Mighty One and coming on the clouds of heaven.'" (Matthew 26:63-64)

After his resurrection, one of his disciples, Thomas, suddenly realizes who Jesus really is, and responds: "My Lord and my God!" (John 20:28). Many times the New Testament acknowledges his divinity,[2] his unique relationship as Son to the Heavenly Father. Christian theologians call this relationship of the Father, Son, and Holy Spirit[3] the Trinity or tri-unity, the three-in-one.[4]

The point here is that Jesus is God in the flesh. When he speaks and teaches, he does so with "all authority on heaven and on earth."[5] But that Jesus would come to earth at all is a huge statement about God's love for us.

## 3. Jesus Atoned for Our Sins on the Cross

The third piece of amazing Good News is that Jesus' death on the cross was not just the tragic martyrdom of a great man. Since Jesus was the Son of God—fully divine—his death provided atonement or payment for our sins. He bore our sins on him and suffered their logical penalty: physical and spiritual death and separation from God the Father.

Seven hundred years before Jesus, the Prophet Isaiah foretold this mission:

[2] For example, Philippians 2:6.
[3] Matthew 28:19.
[4] For more, read my article, "Four Reasons Why I Believe in the Trinity," *Joyful Heart Newsletter*, August 22, 2000 (www.joyfulheart.com/scholar/trinity.htm).
[5] Matthew 28:18.

"Surely he took up our infirmities
and carried our sorrows....
But he was pierced for our transgressions,
he was crushed for our iniquities;
the punishment that brought us peace was upon him,
and by his wounds we are healed....
For he bore the sin of many,
and made intercession for the transgressors." (Isaiah
53:4-5, 12)

Jesus talked about his death in clear terms:

"For even the Son of Man did not come to be served, but
to serve, and to give his life as a ransom for many."
(Mark 10:45)

St. Peter put it this way:

"For Christ died for sins once for all,
the righteous for the unrighteous,
to bring you to God." (1 Peter 3:18a)

Though it is difficult for us to understand, the Bible
teaches that Jesus served as a substitute or stand-in for us.
Jesus did not bear his own sins—he was sinless—but he
bore the punishment that justice requires for our sins.[6]
That is the meaning of the cross. It is terrible to contem-

Francisco de Zurbarán (1598-1664),
"The Crucifixion" (1627), oil on canvas,
290 x 168 cm, Art Institute Museum,
Chicago.

plate, but Good News in the sense that we are forgiven of our sin and guilt. Nothing stands
between us and God now. We are free!

## Last Supper—Lord's Supper

Ever since earliest times, we Christians have remembered Jesus' atoning death for our
sins in a unique way, in a sacrament or ordinance known as the Lord's Supper, eating bread
and drinking wine (or grape juice) together. It commemorates Jesus' last meal with his
disciples (Matthew 26:26-29). The Apostle Paul explained it this way:

"For I received from the Lord what I also passed on to you: The Lord Jesus, on the night
he was betrayed, took bread, and when he had given thanks, he broke it and said, 'This
is my body, which is for you; do this in remembrance of me.'

In the same way, after supper he took the cup, saying, 'This cup is the new covenant in
my blood; do this, whenever you drink it, in remembrance of me.' For whenever you eat
this bread and drink this cup, you proclaim the Lord's death until he comes." (1 Corinthians 11:23-26)

---

[6] You can learn more about the meaning of the crucifixion in two online Bible studies, "Behold, the Lamb of God"
(www.jesuswalk.com/lamb/), also available as a book; and "The Seven Last Words of Christ from the Cross"
(www.jesuswalk.com/7-last-words/), also available as a book.

Today, Christians partake of the Lord's Supper in small, informal gatherings in homes as well as in highly formal settings in huge cathedrals, and all in between. Different Christian traditions call it by different names—communion, the Lord's Table, Eucharist, the Lord's Supper, Mass—and have different customs about how to partake of it. But on two points we all agree:

- The **Bread** reminds us that Jesus' body was broken or given for us.
- The **Cup** reminds us that Jesus' blood was shed for us.

We are never to forget or take lightly Jesus' sacrifice for our sins.[7] It is Good News!

## 4. Jesus Was Raised from the Dead

The fourth piece of amazing Good News is that after Jesus died on the cross, he rose from the dead.

Jesus was not in a coma. He really died. He had been speared in the side to verify his death. Then he was wrapped in grave clothes and placed in a rock tomb, the entrance to which was closed by a very large stone.

> "On the first day of the week, very early in the morning, the women took the spices they had prepared and went to the tomb. They found the stone rolled away from the tomb, but when they entered, they did not find the body of the Lord Jesus. While they were wondering about this, suddenly two men in clothes that gleamed like lightning stood beside them. In their fright the women bowed down with their faces to the ground, but the men said to them, 'Why do you look for the living among the dead? He is not here; he has risen!'" (Luke 24:1-6)

Afterward Jesus appeared to his disciples and many other people. This was not done in secret. There were many credible witnesses, even twenty-five years after the fact. The Apostle Paul wrote:

> "For what I received I passed on to you as of first importance: that Christ died for our sins according to the Scriptures, that he was buried, that he was raised on the third day according to the Scriptures, and that he appeared to Peter, and then to the Twelve. After that, he appeared to more than five hundred of the brothers at the same time, most of whom are still living, though some have fallen asleep." (1 Corinthians 15:3-7)

Jesus was with his disciples for about 40 days after the resurrection. Then Jesus left them in what is called "the Ascension." Ten days later, the Holy Spirit came upon the fledgling church on the Day of Pentecost, which we will discuss in Lesson 7.

Doubters have long disputed the resurrection. "Dead people don't come back to life," they say. But those who have examined the evidence carefully have found that Jesus' resurrection makes more sense than any other explanation. It was a miracle, pure and simple. To say that it is impossible for God to do miracles is silly.

---

[7] You can learn more about the Lord's Supper in my online Bible study, "The Lord's Supper: Eucharist and Communion Meditations for Disciples" (www.jesuswalk.com/lords-supper/), also available as a book.

The implications of this are powerful.

- **Jesus is the only founder of a major religion who is claimed to have been raised from the dead**. This sets him apart from all others. God has authenticated his teaching and his death for our sins by raising him from the dead.
- **Jesus has conquered death**, our ancient enemy. Though we humans die, we follow One who was raised from the dead. Our promise is that our bodies, too, will be raised from the dead on the Last Day.[8]
- **Jesus is alive**. He is present with us today by his Spirit.

## 5. Jesus Lives in Us by His Spirit

The fifth piece of amazing Good News is that Jesus lives within us by his Spirit. We will explore this more fully in Lesson 7. But for now, rejoice that God has made his home in you. Jesus said:

"If anyone loves me, he will obey my teaching. My Father will love him, and **we will come to him and make our home with him**." (John 14:23)

So what is the Good News, the Gospel? We have talked about five audacious claims of the Gospel:

1. God loves you and me.
2. Jesus is God in the flesh.
3. Jesus died on the cross to atone for our sins.
4. Jesus was raised from the dead on the third day.
5. Jesus lives in us by his Spirit

One verse that we looked at already sums up the central truths of this amazing Good News very well:

"For God so loved the world that he gave his one and only Son, that whoever believes in him shall not perish but have eternal life." (John 3:16)

That, indeed, is Good News! That is the Gospel!

## Prayer

Father, thank you for this Good News. Help me to understand it better. Give me joy in this Good News. And help me to share it with others. In Jesus' name, I pray. Amen.

## Participant Guide. 6. Gospel—Understanding Christ's Story

### Memory Verse

"For God so loved the world that he gave his one and only Son, that whoever believes in him shall not perish but have eternal life." (John 3:16, NIV)

---

[8] You can learn more about the resurrection in my online Bible study, "Resurrection and Easter Faith" (www.jesuswalk.com/resurrection/), also available as a book.

## Questions and Discussion Points

1. **Read aloud five times** today's memory verse (John 3:16) and write it on a card.
2. **Discuss.** What does "Gospel" mean?
3. **Discuss.** Which parts of the Gospel are celebrated in the major Christian holidays of Advent, Christmas, Good Friday, Easter, and Pentecost?
4. **Discuss.** What does "incarnation" mean? Why do you think Jesus had to come in the flesh? Why do you think the meaning of Christmas has been so distorted by our culture?
5. **Discuss.** How can Jesus be God? What is Jesus' relationship to the Father and the Spirit?
6. **Discuss.** Why did Jesus have to die on the cross? Why do our sins make us deserving of spiritual death? Who was Jesus that he could take the punishment that we deserve?
7. **Discuss.** Why do you think Jesus was raised from the dead? What are the implications of the resurrection? Why do you think the meaning of Easter has been so distorted by our culture?
8. **Discuss** the Lord's Supper, sometimes called Communion, the Eucharist, the Mass. What is it supposed to remind us of? How is the Lord's Supper practiced in the church you are attending? Have you partaken of the Lord's Supper yet? Why or why not?
9. **Discuss** how your quiet time with God is coming. Are you experiencing any problems here? Have you finished reading one of the Gospels yet?
10. **Discuss** how you are forgiving those who have hurt you? Have you been able to forgive them in your heart yet? If not, what seems to be the problem?
11. **Review your memory verses** from Lesson 1 (Ephesians 2:8-9), Lesson 2 (John 8:31-32), Lesson 3 (1 John 1:9), Lesson 4 (John 13:34-35), and Lesson 5 (1 John 4:7-8). Say them together with your mentor without looking at your cards.
12. **Pray for each other**. Share with your mentor your needs to pray about and ask your mentor how you should pray for him or her. Then spend a few minutes praying for each other aloud.
13. **Appointment**. Set a time and place to meet and go through next week's lesson.

## Outline of Lesson 6. Gospel—Understanding Christ's Story

1. **God Loves Us** (see Lesson 5)
2. **Jesus Is God in the Flesh**
   - This is called "the incarnation."
   - Jesus was born of a virgin (Luke 1:35).
   - He is called Son of God, Savior, Christ/Messiah, the Lord, Son of Man, and God (Luke 1:35; 2:11; Matthew 26:63-64; John 20:28).
   - The three Persons of the Godhead are called the Trinity.
3. **Jesus Atoned for Our Sins on the Cross**
   - Jesus' death provided atonement or payment for our sins (Isaiah 53:4-5, 12; Mark 10:45; 1 Peter 3:18a).
   - Jesus served as a substitute or stand-in for us.
   - The Lord's Supper is the way that we remember Jesus death for our sins (1 Corinthians 11:23-26).
     - The bread reminds us of Jesus body being broken for us.
     - The cup reminds us of Jesus shedding his blood for us.
4. **Jesus Was Raised from the Dead**
   - Jesus died on Good Friday and was raised on the third day, Sunday morning (Luke 24:1-6).
   - Jesus appeared to his disciples and many others after his resurrection (1 Corinthians 15:3-7).
   - The implications of the resurrection are:
     - The resurrection makes Christianity unique.
     - Jesus has conquered death for all of us.
     - Jesus is alive.
5. **Jesus Lives in Us by His Spirit**
   - God has made his home in you (John 14:23).
     More in Lesson 7.

# 7. Holy Spirit—The Power of God's Presence

The Holy Spirit is probably the least understood Person of the Godhead or Trinity. But when you became a Christ-follower, you had already experienced his work. (I am referring to the Holy Spirit a "He," because the Bible talks about him as a Person, not as just an impersonal force.) We are going to spend some time talking about him, because as you understand the dynamic of the Spirit in your life, you will be better able to cooperate with his working in you.

The word "spirit" comes from the word for "breath" or "wind"—unseen, but powerful.

## Convincing Work of the Spirit

The Holy Spirit's work began in you even before you committed your life to Christ. Jesus told his disciples of the Holy Spirit:

> "When he comes, he will convict the world of guilt in regard to sin and righteousness and judgment." (John 16:8)

In Greek, the language in which the New Testament was originally written, the same word can be translated "convict" and "convince." The Spirit both *convinced* you that Jesus was the Way and *convicted* or made you aware of, and ashamed of, your sins.

Likewise, when you tell someone about Christ, you can't "talk them into becoming a Christian." That is the Holy Spirit's responsibility. Instead, relax, trust God, love that person with all your heart, and say what God puts into your mind. Bringing people to faith in Christ is the Holy Spirit's work. You are the assistant, not the other way around.

## Life-Giving Power of the Spirit

Jesus said to Nicodemus, a religious leader who was trying to understand Jesus' teaching:

> "I tell you the truth, no one can enter the kingdom of God unless he is born of water and the Spirit. Flesh gives birth to flesh, but the Spirit gives birth to spirit. You should not be surprised at my saying, 'You must be born again.'" (John 3:5-7)

Some people imagine that being a Christian is primarily believing certain truths and propositions. Truth and faith are involved, of course, but truth itself is not the spark of life, the breath of life. When the Holy Spirit comes into a person, he imparts the life of God and changes the person.

Doesn't Jesus live in a person's heart? Yes. It is the *Spirit* of Jesus that lives in you.

Spirit of Christ = Spirit of God = Holy Spirit

The Holy Spirit is sent by Jesus from the Father to dwell in a person (John 15:26). There is no conflict. The Holy Spirit is God, working in full cooperation with the Father and Son. It's not important to determine exactly whether the Holy Spirit or Jesus is doing something. Just realize that each has his own particular area of ministry.

Christians have struggled for centuries to understand this mystery of the Father, Son, and Holy Spirit. How can they be one, and still be three persons? This is the Trinity or Tri-unity that we mentioned in Lesson 6. They are all equally God, but in some way they act as different Persons. I know that sounds strange, but that is the clear teaching of the Bible.[1]

The point I'm trying to make is that the Holy Spirit in a person makes the difference between being religious, but spiritually dead, and being alive spiritually. The Spirit brings spiritual life. The life of God is a gift, not something a person can "achieve" through believing it so.

## Be Filled with the Spirit

The Spirit is the source of our spiritual life, so in that sense every true Christian has received the Holy Spirit (Romans 8:9). But sometimes, the presence of the Holy Spirit seems to be at low ebb in our lives. St. Paul exhorts us to: "Be filled with the Spirit" (Ephesians 5:18).

The New Testament uses several terms to describe the Spirit in a believer's life:

- **Receive the Holy Spirit**, that is, "take into your possession" the Holy Spirit (John 7:39; Acts 1:8; 2:38; 8:15; 10:47; Galatians 3:2, 14)
- **Be baptized with the Holy Spirit**, that is, "be immersed in" or "be overwhelmed by" the Spirit (Luke 3:16; Acts 1:5; 11:16)
- **Be filled with the Holy Spirit**, that is, "become full" of the Spirit (Acts 2:4; 4:8, 31; 9:17; 13:57; Ephesians 5:18)

In many cases, these words are used synonymously. Sometimes in Scripture we read about various supernatural phenomena that accompany this initial filling of the Spirit; other places we don't. Of course, we don't seek an experience, but the Spirit Himself.

The point is that we seek to be filled with the Holy Spirit's power at all times—not just a taste, but the fullness. We experience this fullness by yielding ourselves and our will to God and to his Holy Spirit.

## The Spirit Helps Us Resist Temptation

Another way the fullness of the Spirit is described in the Bible is as "walking" or "living" in the Spirit or "being led" by the Spirit. In Lesson 3 we talked about resisting temptation. The Holy Spirit plays an important role here, too.

---

[1] For more on this, read my article, "Four Reasons Why I Believe in the Trinity," *Joyful Heart Newsletter*, August 22, 2000 (www.joyfulheart.com/scholar/trinity.htm).

"But I say, **walk by the Spirit**, and do not gratify the desires of the flesh. For the desires of the flesh are against the Spirit, and the desires of the Spirit are against the flesh; for these are opposed to each other, to prevent you from doing what you would. But if you are **led by the Spirit** you are not under the law." (Galatians 5:16-18, RSV)

"Living" or "walking" by the Spirit is the key. It is not focusing on the sins that plague us and resisting them toe-to-toe. Rather, it is yielding ourselves to the Spirit and asking him for help to resist. If we focus on the temptation, we are likely to fall. But if we turn our focus to the Spirit, we will be able to stand firm.

## Fruit of the Spirit

Not only does the Holy Spirit bring the spark of spiritual life to you, he also works in you to make you more like Jesus.

"The **fruit of the Spirit** is love, joy, peace, patience, kindness, goodness, faithfulness, gentleness and self-control. Against such things there is no law." (Galatians 5:22-23)

A tree produces fruit if it is well-watered and healthy. If the tree is sickly, the blossoms will be few and the fruit shriveled. The Holy Spirit works within you to build the qualities of Christ's character in you.

As you yield to the Holy Spirit, your character gradually changes. Don't be disappointed if this doesn't happen overnight. Yes, some lifestyle changes will take place quickly and dramatically.

Our basic character is different. It is the product of many years of attitudes and decisions. And as we mentioned in Lesson 5 on love, our character before Christ is primarily centered on self-interest, not genuine love—love for God and love for others.

However, the Holy Spirit works with us to chip away at the old nature and replace it with the fruit or product of the Spirit's activity, beginning with love.

## Gifts of the Spirit

Here is an aspect of the Holy Spirit that is exciting: the gifts of the Spirit—powerful spiritual equipment to carry out Christ's mission. Notice the difference:

- Fruit of the Spirit—the *character* of Christ formed in us
- Gifts of the Spirit—*spiritual equipment* for our mission

Both are important. One without the other produces an impotent Christian.

God has so "wired" each of us that each of us has talents, abilities, passions, and special spiritual empowerments to help God's work.

"There are different kinds of gifts, but the same Spirit. There are different kinds of service, but the same Lord. There are different kinds of working, but the same God works all of them in all men. Now to each one the manifestation of the Spirit is given for the common good." (1 Corinthians 12:4-7)

Let's look briefly at a few of the gifts that the Holy Spirit bestows, though the list below is by no means complete.

- **Teaching** is a gift of the Spirit to communicate God's truths effectively (Ephesians 4:11; Romans 12:7b).
- **Pastoring** is a gift that enables a person to lead and care for God's people (Ephesians 4:11).
- **Evangelism** is a gift that helps a person communicate the Gospel effectively and win people to Christ. This is beyond simple witnessing which we are all expected to do, but a special gift (Ephesians 4:11; Acts 8:12, 26-39; 21:8).
- **Music and Artistic Skills** are spiritual gifts to be used for God, too (Exodus 31:3; 1 Chronicles 25:7).
- **Service**[2] is a spiritual gift. We are all called to serve, but some have the special spiritual gift of assisting another person in God's work, filling in behind the scenes (Romans 12:7a; 1 Corinthians 12:28).
- **Mercy**, that is, an extraordinary empathy for others, is a special gift used by God, often by those who have a healing ministry (Romans 12:8d).
- **Encouragement or exhortation** is a gift that God uses to call others to their best in the Lord (Romans 12:8a).

We may look at these as "natural" gifts, but they're not just ordinary. They are empowered spiritually. The Bible also talks about some gifts that we would classify as "supernatural": gifts of healing and miracles, prophecy and a word of knowledge, for example (1 Corinthians 12:28).

Through powerful gifts of the Holy Spirit, lives have been changed, churches have been renewed, nations have been transformed. It is hard to overestimate the power of God working through a spiritually-gifted individual who is in tune with the Spirit.

The primary lists of spiritual gifts are found in 1 Corinthians 12; Romans 12:4-8; and 1 Peter 4:7-11. Various people have counted the spiritual gifts mentioned in the Bible and come up with numbers like 9, 19, 27, etc. But I think that though the *categories* of gifts may be limited, the *expression* of those gifts are as infinite and unique as there are people. A better term might be "gift mix," since God mixes our spiritual gift or gifts with the personalities and passions he gave us.

## Discovering Your Spiritual Gifts

One of your tasks as a new Christ-follower is to begin to discover the spiritual gifts that God has given you, and then use them for God. But be patient. It might take a while to get a good idea of how God has gifted you.

Try different kinds of ministries to see which you do best. You will be most effective in the areas where you have a spiritual gift. You will find that other believers will confirm your

---

[2] The gift of service is sometimes called the gift of "helps," as it is translated in the KJV, 1 Corinthians 12:28.

ministry in certain areas. You are also likely to find great joy and fulfillment in the areas where you have a spiritual gift. Sometimes taking a written "spiritual gifts inventory" will help you identify these areas. Ask your pastor about this.

When you discover the areas where you have the strongest spiritual gifts, concentrate your time and efforts there for greatest effectiveness for Christ's kingdom.

## Nothing Is Impossible

We are so used to living in the natural world that is ruled by the physical laws God has set in place, that it is hard for us to lift our faith beyond them. But realize that the Holy Spirit is God living inside of you, filling you. Because this is true, nothing is impossible—nothing!

**To Jeremiah:** "I am the LORD, the God of all mankind. Is anything too hard for me?" (Jeremiah 32:27)

**Angel Gabriel:** "For nothing is impossible with God." (Luke 1:37)

**Jesus:** "What is impossible with men is possible with God." (Luke 18:27)

**Jesus:** "I tell you the truth, if you have faith as small as a mustard seed, you can say to this mountain, 'Move from here to there' and it will move. Nothing will be impossible for you." (Matthew 17:20)

## Walking in the Spirit

When you are walking with a portable radio, sometimes you have to adjust the antenna and retune the station to get the best signal. In the same way, learn to walk with the Holy Spirit, constantly seeking to stay attuned to his voice.

"If we live by the Spirit, let us also **walk** by the Spirit." (Galatians 5:25, RSV)

We believers have an immense privilege: to have God live within our bodies by his Spirit and to be able to follow the guidance of the Holy Spirit. These are more than words. They are a reality.

So I encourage you to press into God, get to know him, learn how his Spirit works. There is absolutely no limit to what God can do with a person who loves him and seeks him.

## Prayer

Lord, my faith is often too small. Break open my faith so that I might see you clearly and learn to trust your Holy Spirit to work through me powerfully. Form Jesus in me, I pray, as I seek to walk by the Spirit. In his name, I pray. Amen.

## Participant Guide: 7. Holy Spirit—The Power of God's Presence

### Memory Verse

"And I will ask the Father, and he will give you another Counselor to be with you forever—the Spirit of truth. The world cannot accept him, because it neither sees him nor knows him. But you know him, for he lives with you and will be in you." (John 14:16-17, NIV)

### Questions and Discussion Points

Note for the Mentor: This lesson is a bit harder to grasp, though the principles are simple and basic. Why don't you ask your pastor to join you for this lesson, if that's possible.

1. **Read aloud five times** today's memory verse (John 14:16-17) and write it on a card.
2. **Discuss**. Why is the Holy Spirit harder to visualize than the Father and the Son? What do you think is the significance of "Spirit" as breath or wind?
3. **Discuss.** Before you were a Christian, did you ever sense the Holy Spirit drawing you to Christ, convicting you of your sins, or convincing you of the truth of Jesus?
4. **Discuss.** How does walking closely with the Spirit help you when you're tempted?
5. **Discuss.** Have you noticed any change in your character and values since you've become a Christian? Which of the fruits of the Spirit mentioned in Galatians 5:22-23 have begun to show up in your character so far?
6. **Discuss.** What gifts of the Spirit does your mentor think he or she has? What gifts of the Spirit do you suspect that you might have?
7. **Discuss.** Why is it so important to discern what gift or gifts you have and then spend time and energy there?
8. **Discuss.** Why do you think we are so quick to think things are impossible? If God is living with you by his Spirit, is there anything impossible to you?
9. **Review your memory verses** from Lesson 1 (Ephesians 2:8-9), Lesson 2 (John 8:31-32), Lesson 3 (1 John 1:9), Lesson 4 (John 13:34-35), Lesson 5 (1 John 4:7-8), and Lesson 6 (John 3:16). Try to say them together with your mentor without looking at your cards.
10. **Pray for each other**. Share with your mentor your needs to pray about and ask your mentor how you should pray for him or her. Then spend a few minutes praying for each other aloud.
11. **Appointment**. Set a time and place to meet and go through next week's lesson.

## Outline of Lesson 7. Holy Spirit—The Power of God's Presence

1. **The Holy Spirit's Nature**
   - The Holy Spirit is a Person, not an impersonal force.
   - The word "Spirit" means "breath" or "wind," unseen, but powerful.
2. **The Holy Spirit Works in Us**
   - The Spirit convinces or convicts people of sin (John 16:8).
   - The Spirit brings spiritual life (John 3:5-7).
     - o  The Spirit dwells in us.
     - o  Spirit of Christ = Spirit of God = Holy Spirit
   - The Spirit fills us. Three phrases are used:
     - o  Receive the Holy Spirit
     - o  Be baptized with the Holy Spirit
     - o  Be filled with the Holy Spirit
   - The Spirit produces fruit and character of Christ in our lives (Galatians 5:22-23).
3. **The Gifts of the Holy Spirit**
   - The Spirit gives each Christian gifts to build up the church and do Christ's work on earth and (1 Corinthians 12:4-7).
   - These gifts include: teaching, pastoring, evangelism, music and artistic skills, service, mercy, and encouragement or exhortation.
   - The Spirit also gives supernatural gifts.
   - You discover your spiritual gifts by trying different ministries and receiving confirmation from others.
4. **The Power of the Holy Spirit**
   - Because the Holy Spirit is God living in us, nothing is impossible (Jeremiah 32:27; Luke 1:37; 18:27; Matthew 17:20).
   - We must seek to walk by the Spirit (Galatians 5:25) and keep our lives attuned to God.

# 8. Witness—Sharing Your Faith

Once you have become a Christ-follower, one of the most natural things you can do is to tell other people what Christ has done for you. This is how the Christian faith spread in the early days to the farthest reaches of the world. People whom Christ had rescued and helped began to spread the word, the Good News, to others that there is help for them, too.

## Witness

The Bible often uses the word "witness," that is, someone who is able to testify to what he or she has seen and experienced personally.

If you were a witness in a court of law, you would be asked to describe what you saw, what you experienced. If you tried to tell about what someone *else* had said about it—beyond your own *personal* experience—you would be told it was hearsay and not admissible.

Why? Because people can hold a wide variety of beliefs—whether they are true or not. But what has happened to them personally, their story, that is something about which they are "expert witnesses."

When you met Christ and he rescued you, your life began to change, perhaps radically. Your story, your testimony, of what things were like with you before, what happened to you when you found Christ, and what has been different since then—that will often interest people. They won't argue with your story. You are the expert on your own life. Often they'll listen.

We will come back to your witness or your personal testimony in a moment.

## The Great Commission

One of the last instructions that Jesus gave to his disciples is known as "The Great Commission"—our marching orders.

"Therefore go and **make disciples** of all nations, **baptizing** them in the name of the Father and of the Son and of the Holy Spirit, and **teaching** them to obey everything I have commanded you. And surely I am with you always, to the very end of the age." (Matthew 28:19-20)

Jesus also gave his disciples this promise:

"You will receive power when the Holy Spirit comes on you; and you will be **my witnesses** in Jerusalem, and in all Judea and Samaria, and to the ends of the earth." (Acts 1:8)

Since they had seen Jesus in action personally and had heard his teachings with their own ears, they were credible "witnesses" to their world and beyond.

## Mapping Your World

What is your world? Who are the people whom God has put around you to love, to pray for, and perhaps to be a witness before?

| | |
|---|---|
| Friends | |
| Family | |
| Work or school associates | |
| Neighborhood or store personnel | |
| Recreation, clubs, teams | |

Why don't you take a few minutes to fill in two or three names of people whom you know in each category—especially people who you would guess aren't committed Christians at this point in their lives.

This is not a "hit list" but rather a "love list"—a list of people with whom you have some influence. This list will remind you to:

1.  **Pray for them.** God will hear your prayers for them and work in their lives. If you love them enough to pray for them, they'll know you love them when you talk with them about Jesus.
2.  **Introduce them** to your Christian friends.
3.  **Invite them to your baptism**, if that is coming up. Having them witness your commitment to Christ can be a powerful way to introduce them to God at work.
4.  **Look for opportunities to share your witness**. Because you are praying, the Holy Spirit will be working in their lives. Sometimes these opportunities come in the form of an extended conversation. Often they come when your friend mentions problems that are going on in his or her life. Remember, however, God hasn't put you there to fix your friend's problems, but to be a loving listener.

Possible outcomes of listening to a friend's problems and needs could be to:

- **Share** how God has helped you when you have been in trouble, and plant the thought that God can help them, too.
- **Offer to pray for them**. If your friend knows you care enough to pray—and that you have a spiritual side that believes in prayer—he or she may open up even more. But don't forget the power of prayer. As you pray, God will answer your prayer for your friend.

  Ask: "Is it okay if I pray for you?" If that is okay with your friend—and you feel comfortable with this—bow your head and speak out your prayer for your friend. If that doesn't seem the thing to do, pray for your friend during the week. Then, next time you see your friend, say, "How are things going since we talked? I have been praying for you." God may surprise you!

## Prepare Your Testimony

When God gives you an opportunity to share what Jesus has done for you, it is very helpful if you have thought ahead of time what to say. That way your testimony can be more clearly communicated. Here is the typical structure of an effective testimony:

1. **This is what my life was like *before* I met Jesus**. Share how you used to be and problems you were experiencing. Often the person you are talking to will begin to identify with some of these same problems.
2. **This is *how* I met Jesus**. These are the circumstances. This is how I came to the place of saying "yes" to him. Explain what happened.
3. **These are the differences in my life *since* I met Jesus**. Do not be afraid to admit that God is still working on you and you are not perfect. But share some of the clear changes you have seen so far.

You will find it very helpful to write down your testimony—using this outline—on one or two sides of a page. Yes, it is work, but it will help clarify things for you.

Your testimony shouldn't be phony or contrived. You don't want to memorize it. But you will find it helps to write it down and practice saying it to someone. That way, when it comes time to tell someone "for real," you will be much more comfortable in doing so.

Being able to share it in just three minutes is a good goal to aim for. That will help you cut it down to the important elements. You can always elaborate, if you need to in a particular witnessing situation.

You may find that when you share your testimony "live" to a non-Christian friend, it comes out differently than you had planned. That is okay! It is probably the Holy Spirit working to fine-tune your testimony to speak to this particular friend's needs.

## The Holy Spirit and Witnessing

The Holy Spirit is your internal guide in witnessing, too. God can "speak" to you through the Holy Spirit. Sometimes the Holy Spirit will put a very strong impression on your mind that you should speak to a certain person. Go ahead. Follow through with this. Many times you'll find that the Holy Spirit has been preparing them and that they're ready to hear your testimony of what Jesus has done for you.

Think of yourself as the junior member of a team. The Holy Spirit is the lead player who sets up the shots. But sometimes he'll pass the ball to you. Be ready for this.

## Testimony and the Gospel

There is an important difference between sharing your testimony with a person and sharing the Gospel or Good News with him or her. These are complementary, but different.

- Your **testimony** is what Christ has done *for you*.
- The **Gospel** is explaining what Christ has done *for the person* to whom you are witnessing.

At this point you are learning to share your testimony, which prepares people to hear more. Ask your mentor or pastor to help you to learn to share the Good News itself. There are many simple ways to share it—"The Bridge," the "Four Spiritual Laws," the "Roman Road," to name a few. But for the moment, learn to share your testimony.

## Some Cautions

1. Be careful about **associating with old friends** who will influence you to go back to your old, sinful lifestyle. It is okay to talk with them about Christ. That's good! But remember that you have an enemy who wants to tempt you to sin. Be careful.

2. **Avoid "missionary dating."** Sometimes a Christian guy feels "called" to date a beautiful girl so he can "witness to her"—or vice versa. Because we are sexual beings, too often our Christian love gets mixed up with other desires, and the clarity of our testimony is lost. Be wise.

3. **Be sensitive to people**. Because your values have changed relative to those of your friends, you will probably seem a little weird to them. That is understandable. But remember to love. Don't be pushy, rude, impatient, or judgmental. Remember, it is the Holy Spirit who brings people to God; it is not all up to you. Love is primary here, not "success."

4. **Don't be afraid of not knowing all the answers**. No one expects you to. Just say, "I'll find out about that and then get back to you." Then ask your mentor or pastor to help you answer the question.

5. **Don't be ashamed**. Sometimes we are very aware that people may look down on us as Christians. That is to be expected. Some looked down on Jesus and persecuted him, too. But that did not stop him from his mission. St. Paul says:

   "So don't be ashamed to testify about our Lord, or ashamed of me his prisoner. But join with me in suffering for the gospel, by the power of God." (2 Timothy 1:8)

## The Centrality of Love

The central core of Christianity is love—unselfish, giving, forgiving love. That needs to be our central motivation when we witness to people. I say that because it is easy to fall into wrong motivations.

One of those motivations is pride. "Look at how great I am! I helped a person to Christ!" It truly is exciting when God uses you this way, but be sure to give the true credit and glory to God.

Another motivation can be doctrine. I have heard street preachers whose main message is how people are going to hell. That is true. But most hell-fire and brimstone preachers seem to have too much self-righteousness and judgmentalism, but too little love.

The people who hear us share about Christ need to be able to sense our love for them. If they can't sense our love, then we need to pray until we can love as Christ wants us to.

## The Testimony of Our Lives

The most powerful testimony you have is Christ working in your life to make you into a new person. Jesus said:

> "You are the light of the world. A city on a hill cannot be hidden. Neither do people light a lamp and put it under a bowl. Instead they put it on its stand, and it gives light to everyone in the house. In the same way, let your light shine before men, that they may see your good deeds and praise your Father in heaven." (Matthew 5:14-16)

When your friends see your life changing, they'll be amazed and curious—and probably a bit threatened. This is kind of a three-step process.

1. **Your lifestyle** is undergoing visible transformation. It speaks for itself.
2. **Your words** point to Christ, so people can understand the reason for the transformation. Unless you explain that this is Christ working in you, people will probably assume that you have "got religion"—and miss the power of what is happened. Your explanation is your powerful testimony that points directly to Christ.
3. **Your love** demonstrates Christ's love for the people you are witnessing to.

Don't wait until you are perfect before sharing your testimony with those around you. People don't expect perfection—really. But when they see humility, love, and sincerity they'll be attracted to you—and to your Savior.

## Prayer

Father, I pray that you will use me to help other people find you. Help my life to bring glory to you. When I am fearful of what other people might think, give me strength. Help me to share my testimony of your working in my life with whomever you inspire me to share. Let me be your witness. In Jesus' name, I pray. Amen.

## Participant Guide: 8. Witness—Sharing Your Faith

### Memory Verse

"In the same way, let your light shine before men, that they may see your good deeds and praise your Father in heaven." (Matthew 5:16, NIV)

### Questions and Discussion Points

1.  **Read aloud five times** today's memory verse (Matthew 5:16) and write it on a card.
2.  **Discuss.** What is the difference between sharing your own personal testimony and sharing the Gospel?
3.  **Discuss.** Why do you think a person will be interested in how you became a Christian? What is the power in a person's testimony?
4.  **Who is in your world?** Discuss with your mentor the people God has placed in your world in the following categories:

     a.  Friends

     b.  Family

     c.  Work or school associates

     d.  Neighborhood or store employees

     e.  Recreation, clubs, and teams

     Which of them do you think might need Christ the most?
5.  **Pray** for each of these names with your mentor. Ask God to open their hearts. Ask God to give you an opportunity to talk with each of them.
6.  **Outline your testimony** in these three points.

     a.  *Before* I became a Christian
     b.  *How* I became a Christian
     c.  *Since* I became a Christian

     Briefly share your testimony with your mentor today using this outline.
7.  **Assignment.** This week go home and write out your testimony. Then practice saying it in about three minutes. The next week share it with your mentor.
8.  **Discuss** the dangers with associating with old friends, "missionary dating," lack of love, and being ashamed.
9.  **Discuss.** Why is love so important in your witnessing?
10. **Discuss.** Isn't just living your life all you need to do? Is sharing a verbal testimony really necessary? Why or why not?

11. **Review your memory verses** from Lesson 1 (Ephesians 2:8-9), Lesson 2 (John 8:31-32), Lesson 3 (1 John 1:9), Lesson 4 (John 13:34-35), Lesson 5 (1 John 4:7-8), and Lesson 6 (John 3:16), and Lesson 7 (John 14:16-17). Try to say them together with your mentor without looking at your cards.

12. **Pray for each other**. Share with your mentor your needs to pray about and ask your mentor how you should pray for him or her. Then spend a few minutes praying for each other aloud.

13. **Appointment**. Set a time and place to meet and go through next week's lesson.

## Outline of Lesson 8. Witness—Sharing Your Faith

1. **Witness**
   - A witness tells what he knows by personal experience.
   - The Great Commission commands us to make disciples (Matthew 28:19-20) and be Christ's witnesses to the world (Acts 1:8).

2. **Sharing Your Testimony**
   - Our world is comprised of our friends, family, work or school associates, neighborhood or store personnel, and recreation, clubs, or teams.
   - We list the people in our world to remind us to pray for them, introduce them to our Christian friends, invite them to our baptism, and look for opportunities to encourage them.
   - In times of trouble, share that God can help them and offer to pray for them.
   - Prepare to share your testimony in about 3 minutes, using this structure:
     o My life before Jesus
     o How I met Jesus
     o My life since Jesus
   - Let the Holy Spirit guide you in when to witness. You are the junior member of his team.
   - Sharing your testimony is what Christ has done for you; sharing the Gospel itself is explaining what Christ has done for that person.

3. **Cautions in Witnessing. Problems can arise from:**
   - Associating with old friends who tempt you to go back to your old lifestyle.
   - "Missionary dating" the opposite sex in order to witness to them.
   - Insensitivity to people.
   - Being afraid of not knowing all the answers.
   - Being ashamed of Christ (2 Timothy 1:8).

4. **Authenticity**
   - Love must be our motivation, not pride or self-righteousness.
   - Our lives will be the most powerful testimony that Christ can change a life.

# 9. Worship—Communing with God

We humans desperately need to worship, that is, to come before God to honor him and to draw close to him. Why? Because we need God.

St. Augustine (354-430 AD) said it well: "God, you have made us for yourself, and our hearts are restless till they find their rest in you."[1] Along these lines, Blaise Pascal (1623-1662) observed that there is a God-shaped vacuum in every heart, that can only be filled by God himself.[2]

## External vs. Internal Worship

It is possible to perform acts of worship (such as prayer, Bible reading, giving offerings, singing) in an outward and formal way—just going through the motions. Indeed, that is how many worship.

But merely outward worship is satisfying to neither God nor to us. Jesus quoted the Prophet Isaiah in saying:

> "These people honor me with their lips, but their hearts are far from me." (Matthew 15:8)

He is not talking about the emotional ups and downs that we experience from day to day, but about people who don't really love or care about God.

Sometimes when you come to worship, your heart may seem cold and your thoughts distracted. Enter into worship anyway. Seek to focus your mind on the Lord. The point is to bring your worship before the Lord intentionally, not just going through the motions. Often after a little "spiritual exercise," however, your mind and body will be able to enter into worship wholeheartedly. Your spirit just needed a little warm-up exercise before the Lord.

---

[1] St. Augustine of Hippo, *Confessions* 1.1.
[2] Paraphrase. The actual quote can be found in Blaise Pascal, *Pensees*, #425.

## Style of Worship Services

Different generations and traditions may prefer one style of worship to another; our preferences tend to be heavily influenced by our culture. But the Bible does not spell out one "right" way of worship.

Heart worship has little to do with the various styles and traditions of worship. Formal liturgical church services with readings, responses, and traditional hymns are no more or less heart worship than non-liturgical church services that feature contemporary choruses and people dressing casually. You can enter into heart worship in either style—or just go through the motions.

By all means, you should attend a gathering of Christians every weekend for public worship, as we discussed in Lesson 4. You need to join a church and participate in its worship and ministries to the community.

But your worship shouldn't take place primarily in a church setting. That should be only the tip of the iceberg. Your primary worship should take place day by day as you live out your life before God.

## Offering Worship

True heart worship should fully engage you in communion—that is, a two-way communication between you and God. You will be giving worship *to* God, and receiving blessings *from* God.

First, let's look at some ways of *offering worship*. You don't have to do all of these. They're just some suggestions so that your offering of worship is not just on a single track, but can be more expressive of your heart.

### Praise

Praise involves acknowledging the greatness of our God. Remember the ACTS acronym we looked at in Lesson 2: Adoration / Confession / Thanksgiving / Supplication. Praise is the Adoration part of this.

We don't praise God to stroke his ego or make him more inclined to answer our prayers. We praise him because he is worthy of our praises. Considering his power and majesty, his love and mercy, and all his other attributes, it is appropriate to offer praise. The book of Psalms—which has served as a songbook, not only for Jews, but also for Christians—gives us many examples of this.

> "I will exalt you, my God the King;
> I will praise your name forever and ever.
> Every day I will praise you
> and extol your name forever and ever.
> Great is the LORD and most worthy of praise;
> his greatness no one can fathom." (Psalm 145:1-3)

Praise is a way of "enthroning" Christ as King (Psalm 22:3), of acknowledging his rightful place as our Lord and God.

If you think about it, praise is the language of faith. When we speak praise to God—even when we are going through difficult times—we are demonstrating our love for and trust in God. Praise can be on our lips throughout the day, not just during our accustomed times of worship.

When you are alone, try shouting to God: "Praise you, Lord!" or some other word of praise. Don't limit your praises to just the domesticated variety. Let your spirit express your love in whatever way seems appropriate at the time.

## Singing

God's Spirit has inspired many thousands of hymns and songs, which have helped Christians lift their praise to God and honor him by telling of his greatness. The lyrics combined with beautiful melodies have a way of helping us express ourselves to God on many levels—with our mind as well as with our emotions.

When Christians sing together in a larger meeting, the presence of everyone joining together in worship and praise helps us express our corporate love for God. It is often inspiring to us. And God looks upon such heart-felt worship with pleasure.

But don't limit your singing only to church gatherings. Begin to sing to the Lord at home, on your way to work. It doesn't really matter whether or not you can carry a tune—just sing. You will find it helps you offer worship to God.

## Thanksgiving

We talked about the importance of thanksgiving as the "T" in the ACTS memory device. Thanking God for what he has done is just basic gratitude, as well as an act of worship and honor. It should be a regular part of your personal worship.

## Confession

We talked about confession in as the "C" in ACTS, as well as in Lesson 3 about dealing with temptation. Regularly confessing any recent sins that God brings to mind, saying a prayer of repentance, and receiving God's forgiveness is an important part of worship, too.

## Prayers

Our prayers or supplications are the "S" in ACTS. I want to encourage you to make this part of your worship, not just as requests, but "talking over with God" aspects of your life and the challenges you face. Thus prayer becomes a discussion, a dialog, not merely a monologue on your part. I like to talk to God about my life as I take a walk. Of course, there will be requests that you are asking God for, too.

## Tithes and Offerings

Perhaps you have thought that the offering plate at church was a kind of embarrassment. It is not. We Christians see giving towards God's work as part of our worship of him. More on that in Lesson 11.

## Offering Thanksgiving before Meals

Since ancient times, believers have used the occasion of eating as a time to give thanks to God. Though you will often hear Christians blessing the *food itself*, the Old Testament and New Testament practice was to *bless and praise God* before eating. Make your meals a time to worship God.

## The Conduct of Your Life

There are many other elements of offering Christian worship. But in a real way, the Bible tells us that the very way you live your life is "your spiritual act of worship" (Romans 12:1, NIV).

## Postures in Worship

Different churches have different traditions of postures in prayer and worship. There are no rules or requirements here, but you may find some of these helpful to you personally in your own quiet time with God:

- **Bowed head** shows reverence before God. But you may also find it helpful to look up to pray.
- **Folded hands** during prayer I think was more an invention of parents trying to keep children from fidgeting during prayer. But if folding your hands helps you pray attentively, that's great.
- **Eyes closed** during prayer can cut down distractions. But it may induce sleep. And don't close your eyes while praying during driving a car or riding a bicycle.
- **Lifted or outstretched hands** has a long history in the Bible as a prayer posture.[3] Many find this meaningful (though in some congregations, people may think you are a radical if you lift your hands). Palms open to God can express requesting or openness. Hands lifted heavenward can be a sign of praise or adoration.
- **Kneeling** is a customary prayer posture in many homes. Some churches have built-in "kneelers" for worshippers to use during prayer.
- **Lying prostrate** on the floor is found in some traditions and can represent full surrender before God. It is seen in the service to ordain priests in the Roman Catholic tradition.
- **Making the sign of the cross** is practiced in many churches. While some people may cross themselves superstitiously, others do this reverently as an act of worship. The sign of the cross is usually made by touching the hand sequentially to the forehead, chest, then each shoulder.

---

[3] See my article, "Lifting Hands in Worship," *Paraclete*, Winter 1986, pp. 4-8. www.joyfulheart.com/scholar/hands.htm

You will find many other postures and acts of worship in the Scriptures, including dancing (2 Samuel 6:14), clapping (Psalm 47:1), and leaping (Luke 6:23).

I mention these postures in worship for two reasons.

1. **Explore.** First, to help you explore various ways that you can express yourself to God in your own personal worship. Try some of these postures. You may find they help.
2. **Understand.** And second, to help you understand worship practices that you may have observed in others. Christians have developed various worship traditions over the years, different for people in different areas of the world and different histories. We can learn from one another.

## Receiving During Worship

We have looked at ways to offer worship to God. Now let's consider ways that we receive during our times of communing with God.

Let me emphasize: We don't worship for what we can get out of it. That is selfishness, not true worship. We worship because God is worthy. But, having said that, we do receive much as we worship—since God intends us to.

## Instruction

Most corporate worship services have a period of instruction, called variously a sermon, message, or homily. The point is not the eloquence of the preacher, but what God wants to say to you personally during this time. His Holy Spirit is active with the Word of God to help you grow. Listen for God's voice to you during this time.

During your own quiet times of worship and meditation you are also seeking God to teach you. That is why you read a passage from the Bible.

## Guidance

Closely related to instruction is guidance for our own personal lives. Sometimes when we are seeking what we should do, God will speak to us during a worship time, since it is then that our hearts are particularly focused on God. This has happened to me many times. Often what God will speak to me has little to do with the speaker's message. But God's own message is imprinted in my thoughts and in my heart.

Besides vocal worship through singing and prayer, I encourage you to let yourself become quiet before God. Sit before him and listen. Often he will drop a word or two into your heart that are just for you. You see, worship is a time of communion between you and God. Your life with the Lord is meant to be a conversation, a dialog, back and forth between you and God.

## Comfort

Our times of worship are meant to stir us up in the Lord, but also to provide comfort to us in the struggles we are experiencing in our lives. When you come to worship, let the presence of God envelop you in comfort and peace.

## Joy

A final blessing of worship is joy—joy in the presence of the Lord. I didn't always experience joy when I was young in the Lord, probably because I hadn't yet learned the practice of praise. But now, again and again, I find a gentle joy in the Lord during my worship. It is a part of the love for God that the Holy Spirit is growing in my heart.

## Emotional Deadness Sometimes

Realistically, we don't always hear God or feel much comfort. Our hearts may be distracted when we come to worship. At times, we may be going through depression when we experience little joy.

Sometimes our worship and devotion seem dead, empty of any spiritual life—at least that is the way we *feel*. But since we worship because God is worthy, not as an emotional pick-me-up, we continue to worship God no matter what our emotions are like at the time.

In normal times, however, as we learn to quiet our hearts before him, the worship we offer to God will be from our hearts, and the blessings we receive from worshipping him will infuse our beings with a sense of his holy presence.

## Regular Worship as a Good Habit

The Gospels show us Jesus' own example of prayer and regular worship:

"Jesus **often** withdrew to lonely places and prayed." (Luke 5:16)

"When he came to Nazareth, where he had been brought up, he went to the synagogue on the Sabbath day, **as was his custom**." (Luke 4:16, NRSV)

For Jesus, praying each day and gathering regularly with others for worship and Scripture reading on the Sabbath was a good habit that was essential to nourish his relationship with the Father while he was here on earth.

It is easy to get out of the habit of worship—both in our own daily quiet times and even worship with the Body of Christ on the weekend. Resist the temptation to neglect worship. Satan seeks to weaken you by starving you spiritually. He can't grab you out of God's hand, but he can pull you away from regular fellowship with God, and so weaken and neutralize your joy, peace, witness, and effectiveness as a child of God.

So make worship central in your life. That is the practice of Jesus and this is the way of his disciples.

## Prayer

Father, you are worthy of all our praise. I ask you to help us to give you the honor that is due your name. Teach us to worship you. Teach us how to praise you. Teach us to listen to you and pour out our hearts to you. Make this channel of communication between us strong and well used. In Jesus' name, we pray. Amen.

## Participant Guide: 9. Worship—Communing with God

### Memory Verse

"I will bless the Lord at all times; his praise shall continually be in my mouth." (Psalms 34:1, NRSV)

### Questions and Discussion Points

1.  **Read aloud five times** today's memory verse (Psalm 34:1) and write it on a card.
2.  **Discuss.** What is the difference between outward worship and worship with your heart? What can we do when our heart seems cold when we come to worship?
3.  **Discuss.** Do we worship out of self-interest or to honor God? What is the problem when we come to worship in order to *get* something, rather than to *offer* something to God?
4.  **Discuss.** Which part of a worship service do you enjoy the most? Why? Which part of a worship service do you think is most honoring to God? Why?
5.  **Discuss.** Which postures have you observed in people who are worshipping? Which have you tried out yourself? Which of these seems most meaningful to you?
6.  **Assignment.** This week in your own personal quiet time, experiment with six or more postures in worship. Then report back next week on what you experienced.
7.  **Discuss.** Have you ever experienced joy in worship? If so, why do you think it brings you joy? Why do you think worship brings God joy?
8.  **Review.** Which of your friends are you particularly praying for that they might become Christians? Has God answered your prayers for them in any way you can see at this point?
9.  **Review.** Last week you worked on an outline for your testimony:
    (a) Before I became a Christian,
    (b) How I became a Christian,
    (c) Since I became a Christian.
    Have you written it out yet? Share it with your mentor today, trying to keep it to about three minutes.
10. **Review your memory verses** from Lesson 1 (Ephesians 2:8-9), Lesson 2 (John 8:31-32), Lesson 3 (1 John 1:9), Lesson 4 (John 13:34-35), Lesson 5 (1 John 4:7-8), and Lesson 6 (John 3:16), Lesson 7 (John 14:16-17), and Lesson 8 (Matthew 5:16). Try to say them together with your mentor without looking at your cards.
11. **Pray for each other.** Share with your mentor your needs to pray about and ask your mentor how you should pray for him or her. Then spend a few minutes praying for each other aloud. Also pray for friends you hope to witness to.
12. **Appointment.** Set a time and place to meet and go through next week's lesson.

## Outline of Lesson 9. Worship—Communing with God

1. **The Nature of Worship**
   - Worship means to come before God to honor him and draw close to him.
   - Our worship needs to be from the heart, not just going through religious motions (Matthew 15:8).
   - Worship styles have little to do with heart worship.

2. **Offering Worship can take many forms:**
   - Praise (Psalm 145:1-3)
   - Singing
   - Thanksgiving
   - Confession
   - Prayers or supplications
   - Tithes and offerings
   - Thanks before meals
   - Conduct of your life (Romans 12:1)
   - Postures can express worship. Here are some for you to explore yourself and understand when you see practiced by others:
     - Bowed head
     - Folded hands
     - Eyes closed
     - Lifted or outstretched hands
     - Kneeling
     - Lying prostrate
     - Making the sign of the cross

3. **Receiving During Worship.** We don't worship primarily to receive, but to honor God.
   - But in worship we can receive:
     - Instruction
     - Guidance
     - Comfort
     - Joy
   - Sometimes we experience emotional deadness during worship. In these times we worship by faith, not by feeling.

4. **Worship should be a regular habit for us as it was for Jesus (Luke 5:16; 4:16).**

# 10. Generosity and Service—Love in Action

Since the core of Christianity is found in love, the natural expression of the Christian faith is found in acts of generosity and service to others.

## Love Gives and Serves

Perhaps the best example of loving service is seen in Jesus himself, who said:

> "For even the Son of Man did not come to be served, but **to serve**, and to **give his life** as a ransom for many." (Mark 10:45)

> "For God so loved the world that **he gave** his one and only Son, that whoever believes in him shall not perish but have eternal life." (John 3:16)

Giving is the larger category of which serving is a vital subset. We serve because we are giving of ourselves.

## Generosity Flows from Love

We looked briefly at Jesus' Parable of the Good Samaritan (Luke 10:30-35) in Lesson 5 in order to illustrate that our responsibility to love our neighbor does not end with our own family or even our own ethnic group. The Samaritan in the story took pity on the injured man:

> "He went to him and bandaged his wounds, pouring on oil and wine. Then he put the man on his own donkey, took him to an inn and took care of him. The next day he took out two silver coins and gave them to the innkeeper. 'Look after him,' he said, 'and when I return, I will reimburse you for any extra expense you may have.'" (Luke 10:33-35)

It is Jesus' example of generosity above and beyond what might be expected. Generosity flows from love.

## Helping the Poor

Hospitality is another example of generosity. When someone needs love and care, we can be stingy and selfish about providing for them, or be open and generous in our response. The Bible says:

> "Share with God's people who are in need. Practice hospitality." (Romans 12:13)

The Bible is very clear that God has a very special concern for justice and fairness for the poor. He sympathizes with their plight.

"I know that the LORD secures justice for the poor and upholds the cause of the needy." (Psalms 140:12)

People often show generosity for selfish reasons—tax benefits, having a building named after them, public recognition, etc. But caring for the poor is another example of the kind of generosity God expects from us. Jesus taught his disciples:

"When you give to the needy, do not let your left hand know what your right hand is doing, so that your giving may be in secret. Then your Father, who sees what is done in secret, will reward you." (Matthew 6:3-4)

St. James said:

"Religion that God our Father accepts as pure and faultless is this: to look after orphans and widows in their distress and to keep oneself from being polluted by the world." (James 1:27)

The reason caring for the poor is at the heart of true religion, is that the poor can't do anything to repay us. Therefore, we help out of actual love, rather than because of what we can get out of it.

## Justice for All

Because of the strong teaching of Scripture, Christians have often been at the forefront of the struggles for social justice, such as the abolition of slavery, the right of all citizens to vote, justice for the poor, to name just a few. This pleases God, who is known as the Defender and Helper of the fatherless (Proverbs 23:10-11; Psalm 10:14).

Jesus saw his ministry, in the words of Isaiah the prophet, as follows:

"The Spirit of the Lord is on me,
because he has anointed me
to preach good news to the poor.
He has sent me to proclaim
freedom for the prisoners
and recovery of sight for the blind,
to release the oppressed,
to proclaim the year of the Lord's favor."
(Luke 4:18-19, quoting Isaiah 61:1-2)

When the Kingdom of God comes in completeness, it will be a kingdom of justice and peace for all. In the meantime, we are to serve in our communities to bring a foretaste of that Kingdom to our world.

## Generosity towards God's Work

From ancient times, believers have contributed toward the work and mission of the church. In the Old Testament, even before Christ, people set aside 10% of their income to the Lord. Ten percent is called a "tithe." Before Jesus, the tithe went to keep the temple in repair, to provide for the priests, to help the poor, and to celebrate before the Lord in worship.

While we are not under Old Testament law, most practicing Christians believe that a tithe of our income should still be given to the Lord for his work in the New Testament era.[1] Ten per cent is still a good guideline, even if it is not a law. This shows generosity toward God and his work.

## Tithing—The Principle of Percentage Giving

I grew up in a Christian home where my parents taught me to tithe my allowance. For every one dollar I received, I set aside ten cents to give to the Lord. Now that I am an adult, the amounts are considerably larger, but the principle of percentage giving remains.

Here is a challenge from God in the Old Testament through the Prophet Malachi:

"Will a man rob God? Yet you rob me. But you ask, 'How do we rob you?' In tithes and offerings. You are under a curse—the whole nation of you—because you are robbing me. Bring the whole tithe into the storehouse, that there may be food in my house.[2]

Test me in this," says the LORD Almighty, "and see if I will not throw open the floodgates of heaven and pour out so much blessing that you will not have room enough for it." (Malachi 3:8-10)

## The Blessings of Tithing

Notice the amazing promise. God says, "Test me in this," and promises to pour out abundant blessing on those who tithe. We see the same kind of promises in the New Testament. Jesus said:

"Give, and it will be given to you.
A good measure, pressed down,
shaken together and running over,
will be poured into your lap.
For with the measure you use,
it will be measured to you." (Luke 6:38)

Someone said it this way: "You can't out-give God." That is true. But, of course, we don't give in order to receive or to become wealthy. That is selfishness. We give because we love God!

I must say that I enjoy giving to God. For me it is worship. And over the years God has blessed me so that I could tithe. It hasn't always been easy. I've had some pretty lean years. But I have also seen God's wonderful provision. I have never been able to out-give God.

---

[1] For more on the topic of tithing, study the Scripture passages mentioned in my article, "Does Your Church Run a Spiritual Sweatshop?" *The Joyful Heart*, October 27, 1997. www.joyfulheart.com/church/sweatshop.htm

[2] "That there may be food in my house," means that there should be food to provide for the temple priests and their families.

## Financial Responsibilities

Of course, God expects us to take care of our financial obligations and the needs of our family. But in doing so, we are not to neglect our responsibility to give to God's work. In fact, giving is part of our worship, as discussed in Lesson 9.

It is not easy to tithe. It is a sacrifice. For example, before being able to tithe fully, you might need to pay off some of the debts you accrued in acquiring nice things. But getting your priorities straightened out is a good thing. Even if you can't start giving 10%, start where you can—2% or 5%—and then work up year by year until you reach the tithe.

## God Is the Owner, We Are Managers

When we think of our property and money as our own, it is easy to resent tithing as a kind of a tax. But consider this verse:

> "The earth is the LORD's, and everything in it,
> the world, and all who live in it." (Psalms 24:1)

We acknowledge that everything we possess really belongs to God. We are not owners, but managers, caretakers, or stewards of what God has entrusted to us for a time. With that mindset, giving back a tithe to God is a joy. If you have time, read Jesus' Parable of the Ten Pounds (Luke 19:11-27) to better understand this view of stewardship of God's property.

We are also caretakers of God's earth. At the beginning of time, God gave Adam and Eve a commission to care for his creation:

> "The LORD God took the man and put him in the Garden of Eden to work it and take
> care of it." (Genesis 2:15)

This is one reason that we Christians take responsibility for the ecology of our cities as well as our planet. We are caretakers of what God has entrusted to us. *He* is the Creator and Owner. We are not!

## Serving Is Another Way of Showing Generosity

One of the key ideas for Jesus was serving.

At the Last Supper, the last meal Jesus had with his disciples before his crucifixion, Jesus knelt down at the feet of each of his twelve disciples and washed their feet. It was a radical act. People just didn't act this way! In Jesus' culture, a host would provide water for a guest to wash his own feet near the door, but he did not do it for them.

But Jesus took the role of a servant and gently washed the feet of each of his disciples. It was a lesson in humility and service that none of them would forget. Afterward, Jesus said:

> "Do you understand what I have done for you? You call me 'Teacher' and 'Lord,' and
> rightly so, for that is what I am. Now that I, your Lord and Teacher, have washed your
> feet, you also should wash one another's feet. I have set you an example that you should
> do as I have done for you." (John 13:12-15)

Serving is an act of humility that characterized Jesus' whole approach. Jesus came as a servant. We also are called to serve others, not with pride, but with humility. That is the disciple's way.

## The Church Is Like a Body

In Lesson 4, we observed that the church—the assembled believers—are spoken of figuratively as a body. In this analogy, Christ is the head and each of us is a part—a finger, a toe, an eye, a muscle. "Now you are the body of Christ," the Apostle Paul wrote, "and each one of you is a part of it" (1 Corinthians 12:27).

The only way a body can sustain its life is for each part of the body to do its part to serve the whole and work together (Ephesians 4:16).

## Spiritual Gifts Equip Us to Serve

So what is your part in the body of Christ? As we discussed in Lesson 7, the Holy Spirit has given spiritual gifts to each of us. These enable us to serve effectively both the church and the community in which he has placed us. It is God's job to equip us. It is our job to humbly serve using those gifts.

Love gives. Love serves. The natural consequence of making love our number one priority is orienting our lives towards giving and serving. How will God have you serve him in his world?

### Prayer

Father, help me to catch the humble servant's heart that Jesus had. He came to serve us because he loved us. Help me to love like that. I pray that you would replace my natural selfishness with a desire to serve you. Teach me to give to you and to others. Teach me to be like Jesus. In his name, I pray. Amen.

## Participant Guide: 10. Generosity and Service—Love in Action

### Memory Verse

"For even the Son of Man did not come to be served, but to serve, and to give his life as a ransom for many." (Mark 10:45, NIV)

### Questions and Discussion Points

1. **Read aloud five times** today's memory verse (Mark 10:45) and write it on a card.
2. **Discuss.** Why does love require giving and service? What is the logical connection?
3. **Define** the word "generous." Why is love generous rather than stingy?
4. **Discuss.** Why do you think God identifies himself so strongly with justice and grace for the poor, the widows, and the orphans? Why do they so often suffer injustice?
5. **Discuss.** What is our motivation to give financially to God and his work? In what way is our giving an act of worship? In what way does our giving reflect our love?
6. **Define** the word "tithe." How should the principle of percentage giving guide our giving in the New Testament era?
7. **Discuss.** Who is the owner of the world? In what sense does all we have belong to God? If God is owner, then what is our role towards our world and our possessions? How does this affect how well we take care of the earth?
8. **Discuss** with your mentor about giving to God's work. Ask your mentor how he or she determines how much to give? Discuss how you can determine what percentage of your income you can begin to give.
9. **Review.** Last week you were to experiment with six or more postures in worship. What did you discover when you did this? Which worship postures did you find most meaningful to you?
10. **Review.** Have you had an opportunity to share your testimony yet? Do you see anything happening in the lives of the friends you are praying for?
11. **Review your memory verses** from Lesson 1 (Ephesians 2:8-9), Lesson 2 (John 8:31-32), Lesson 3 (1 John 1:9), Lesson 4 (John 13:34-35), Lesson 5 (1 John 4:7-8), and Lesson 6 (John 3:16), Lesson 7 (John 14:16-17), Lesson 8 (Matthew 5:16), and Lesson 9 (Psalms 34:1). Try to say them together with your mentor without looking at your cards.
12. **Pray for each other.** Share with your mentor your needs to pray about and ask your mentor how you should pray for him or her. Then spend a few minutes praying for each other aloud. Also pray for the friends to whom you hope to witness.
13. **Appointment.** Set a time and place to meet and go through next week's lesson.

## Outline of Lesson 10. Generosity and Service—Love in Action

1. **Love is giving and generous**
   - Jesus modeled loving service for us (Mark 10:45; John 3:16).
   - Generosity flows from love, as seen in the Parable of the Good Samaritan (Luke 10:30-35).

2. **Ways We Can Show Generosity**
   - Helping the Poor (Psalms 140:12).
     - o Showing hospitality (Romans 12:13).
     - o Giving to the poor unselfishly (Matthew 6:3-4).
     - o Helping orphans and widows is the essence of genuine religion (James 1:27).
   - Seeking Justice for All
     - o Based on Jesus' understanding of his ministry (Luke 4:18-19).
     - o Extending now blessings that will ultimately come the Kingdom of God is established.

3. **Showing generosity towards God's work**
   - Since ancient times God's people set aside a tithe (10%) for God's work, to help the poor, and to celebrate in worship.
   - We are not under the Old Testament law, but tithing is still a good guideline for our generosity towards God.
   - Tithing, percentage giving, comes with an offer of God's blessing (Malachi 3:8-10; Luke 6:38).
     - o We don't tithe selfishly in order to receive blessings, but out of love for God.
     - o Tithing is a sacrifice, since we are responsible to take care of our other financial obligations.
     - o Start by giving the percentage you are able, then ask God to help you increase to 10%.
   - God is the owner of all; we are managers or stewards (Psalms 24:1; Luke 19:11-27; Genesis 2:15).

4. **Serving is another way of showing generosity**
   - Jesus modeled service when he washed the disciples' feet at the Last Supper (John 13:12-15).
   - Since we are members of the body, the church, each of us must do our part (1 Corinthians 12:27; Ephesians 4:16).
   - Spiritual gifts equip us to serve.

# 11. Bible—Guidebook for Living

Sometimes we get discouraged at the slow pace of our own spiritual growth. But remember that Jesus spent three years with his disciples teaching them, encouraging them, sometimes even rebuking them when they needed it. This is a process, not a speed contest.

Unlike the disciples, we don't have Jesus with us in the flesh. But we do have several powerful aids to our spiritual growth:

1. **Christ's Spirit** lives within us—the Holy Spirit. He reminds us of what Jesus taught and helps to work change within us. We considered his ministry in Lesson 7.
2. **Christian brothers and sisters** are with us to encourage us, teach us, love us, model for us the life of Christ—and rebuke us when we need it. They are part of the family in which we are being raised. This connection is vital to our growth. We considered this in Lesson 4.
3. **The Bible**, God's Word, continues to instruct us, day after day, and conveys to us the teachings of Jesus and his apostles. Though we looked at this briefly in Lesson 2, let's consider this in greater detail today.

## Inspiration of Scripture

As you have probably recognized, the Bible is not just another book. Christians call it Holy Scripture because it has been inspired by the Holy Spirit. Let me explain what we mean by that. The Apostle Paul wrote:

> "All scripture is **inspired by God** and is useful for teaching, for reproof, for correction, and for training in righteousness." (2 Timothy 3:16, NRSV)

The word "inspired" here means, literally, "God-breathed." St. Peter put it slightly differently:

> "No prophecy of Scripture came about by the prophet's own interpretation. For prophecy never had its origin in the will of man, but **men spoke from God** as they were carried along by the **Holy Spirit**." (2 Peter 1:20-21)

When we say that the Bible is inspired, we mean that the Holy Spirit worked to guide each Bible author in the 1,500-year span of time during which the Scriptures were being written.

In most cases, the Holy Spirit did not dictate the words. Rather, the Holy Spirit inspired the writer to record God's message accurately in the writer's own words. But that makes it no less inspired.

Of course, each writer lived in a particular culture at a particular point in history and wrote in a particular language. As we understand what the writer meant to say in his own cultural and historical setting, we can hear God speaking to us.

In some instances, the Spirit has inspired authors to record the history of man's arrogance and disobedience for us to learn from. At other times the Spirit inspired profiles of men and women of faith for us to emulate. The Spirit inspired ancient poets to write songs of praise in the Psalms, and prophets to bring messages from God to correct his people. In the New Testament, the Spirit inspired Paul, Peter, and other apostles to write letters to guide the early church. The Bible contains many varieties of teaching, but all are inspired by the Holy Spirit.

## The Authority of Scripture

Since Scripture is inspired by God, it is authoritative. We believe that the Bible speaks with God's authority to direct our faith and lives in every area about which it teaches.

## Not a Law Book, but a Love Book

Some Christians get pretty legalistic, acting as if the Bible were a law book. It is not. Rather it is God teaching his people how to live. Once Jesus was asked which was the greatest commandment in the Old Testament. Jesus replied:

"'Love the Lord your God with all your heart
and with all your soul
and with all your mind.'
This is the first and greatest commandment.
And the second is like it:
'Love your neighbor as yourself.'
All the Law and the Prophets hang on these two commandments." (Matthew 22:37-40)

These two commands—(1) Love God and (2) Love your neighbor—are the basic commands. The teaching of Jesus and the apostles in the New Testament largely explain how to live out these commands in our everyday lives.

Nevertheless, we are to take Jesus' instruction to his disciples very seriously. We can't reinterpret it "in love" to suit our own desires. Jesus' teaching is authoritative.

But his teaching is also freeing, not some kind of heavy burden on our lives. Jesus told his followers:

"Come to me, all you who are weary and burdened, and I will give you rest. Take my yoke upon you and learn from me, for I am gentle and humble in heart, and you will find rest for your souls. For my yoke is easy and my burden is light." (Matthew 11:28-30)

## Why We Should Read the Bible

I hope that you will develop the life-long habit of reading the Bible. Here's why:

1. **Instruction**. Jesus' teaching is powerful and direct from God. That is why you will want to read the Gospels and the teachings of Jesus' apostles. Otherwise you will be ignorant. Jesus said:

   "If you hold to my teaching, you are really my disciples. Then you will know the truth, and the truth will set you free." (John 8:31-32)

2. **Correction**. Many are the times that I have read something in the Bible that spoke directly to something wrong in my life that needed fixing. The Word brings conviction—and change. I'm a better person for it. The author of Hebrews says:

   "The word of God is living and active. Sharper than any double-edged sword, it penetrates even to dividing soul and spirit, joints and marrow; it judges the thoughts and attitudes of the heart." (Hebrews 4:12)

3. **Examples**. The Bible is full of stories of real people who encountered God and who God used powerfully. You will learn a lot from their successes as well as their mistakes. The Bible includes hundreds of case studies of God working with people.

4. **Training and Growth**. The Bible is a kind of training manual in how to live. As you read and begin to internalize its contents, you will grow stronger and more powerful in the Lord.

5. **Inspiration**. Many times you will be inspired, awed, amazed, when you are reading the Bible. All of a sudden you will see something there—a new insight, a new truth will stand out to you.

## The Holy Spirit Illuminates the Word

The source of these sudden insights and inspirations is the Holy Spirit at work in you. Since the Holy Spirit inspired the Scriptures in the first place, it is not surprising that he will illuminate them to you as well. Trying to read or teach the Bible without the work of the Holy Spirit is like trying to drive a car without oil. The Spirit works with the Word.

## New Testament

Now let me explain a bit about the kinds of books there are in the New Testament. The 27 books and letters are categorized in this way:

**Gospels**              Records of Jesus' life and teachings. There are four: Matthew, Mark, Luke, and John. Start your reading of the Bible here.

| | |
|---|---|
| **Acts of the Apostles** | An exciting history of the early growth of Christianity. |
| **Paul's Letters** | The Apostle Paul was originally a vicious opponent of Christianity until he met Christ in a vision and was radically changed. God used him to spread belief in Jesus all over the Mediterranean region. He was martyred in Rome about 65 AD under Emperor Nero. He wrote about 13 letters that are in our Bibles. |
| **General Letters** | These letters are written by other apostles and early Christian leaders, mainly Peter, James, and John. |
| **Revelation** | This is a unique book designed to give persecuted Christians hope and encouragement about the future. It is filled with symbols that seem bizarre to us, but all of it has powerful meaning when you understand it. Save this for later reading. |

## Translations

Now let me say a word about Bible translations. The Old Testament was written in Hebrew.[1] The New Testament was written in Greek. Bible scholars who have spent their lives studying these languages have translated the Greek and Hebrew manuscripts into English and many other languages. For more on this, see Appendix 3. "How to Select a Bible."

There's a difference, however, between a translation and a paraphrase. A translation seeks to be an accurate rendering of the original language, without going beyond what was said in the original. A paraphrase on the other hand, is freer in its renderings, endeavoring to put the concept into everyday words, often adding ideas that weren't in the original. Here are some examples:

**Translations**

King James Version (KJV, 1611)
New International Version (NIV, 1973, 1983)
New American Standard Bible (NASB, 1977)
New Revised Standard Version (NRSV, 1989)

**Paraphrases**

Living Bible (LB, 1971)
The Message (Msg, 1993)

If you don't already have a Bible, I recommend that you get a good, modern translation—preferably one of the newer translations listed above. If your first language is not English, I encourage you to obtain a Bible in your own language. That way you can learn God's word more easily.

---

[1] A few chapters in Daniel were written in Aramaic, a language similar to Hebrew.

## Study Bible

When you can save up money for one, I recommend that you get a study Bible. This is a Bible that includes lots of notes about hard-to-understand verses and a list of other verses that amplify the same topic of the verse you are reading. In the back you may find a brief Bible dictionary so you can look up topics and a concordance, a kind of index of the Bible by the key word used in some of the Bible's most meaningful verses. You will find that a good study Bible will be a resource that you can use for many years to help you learn the Bible better.

## Daily Bible Reading

As I mentioned in Lesson 2, one of the most important disciplines you can develop is that of daily Bible reading. Setting aside 5 to 10 minutes each day for a quiet time in which to read the Bible and pray will literally change your life and supercharge your growth in faith.

Here are a couple of Bible reading plans:

**New Testament, one chapter a day**: Remember that chapters are relatively short. You can probably read a chapter in five minutes or less. Start in the Gospels and work through to Revelation. Since the New Testament has 260 chapters (some shorter, some longer), you will get through the entire New Testament a little more than once each year. This is a great place for you to start.

**Three Bible chapters a day**: When you have grown some as a Christ-follower, you will want to add the Old Testament to your daily reading. This takes about 10 minutes on most days—a bit more with longer chapters. Here is a "balanced diet":

- **The Psalms** are the praise and prayer book of the Bible, so I read one of these each day. There are 150 Psalms or chapters, so you will get through the Psalms twice in a year.
- **The Old Testament** contains 929 chapters (minus the 150 chapters in Psalms). That leaves you 779 chapters. You will get through the Old Testament once every two years.
- **The New Testament** contains 260 chapters, so you get through it in less than a year.

If you'd like to print out a daily Bible reading guide that you can tuck into your Bible, you can find links to several Bible reading plans online.

www.jesuswalk.com/beginning/bible-reading-plans.htm

## When the Bible Seems Boring

Sometimes when you sit down to read the Bible it will seem boring—you just can't get into it, or your mind glides over the surface so you can't even remember what you have just read. Sometimes your spirit will be sluggish or your mind tired. Do not be too hard on yourself. "The spirit is willing but the flesh is weak."[2]

---

[2] Matthew 26:41.

Try making some changes. Pray aloud before you read. Change your position: stand up or kneel rather than sitting. Read less that day or study a single verse or paragraph. I have found that reading aloud helps me concentrate when I'm distracted.

Yes, some days you won't seem to get much out of your Bible reading time, but keep at it. Over time you will find that regular Bible reading will change your life.

## Scripture Memory

During *JesusWalk: Beginning the Journey* I have asked you to memorize one key verse each week. Even though Scripture memory may seem difficult at first, keep at it. Find a verse that speaks to you and commit it to memory. Write it down on a paper or card and tape it to the wall or a mirror where you will see it often. Say it aloud—first reading it, then saying it from memory as you are able, only looking when you forget a word or phrase. Then occasionally review the verses you've learned.

The value in Scripture memory is that you will always have God's word in your head—even if you don't have your Bible handy. You will find this especially helpful in times of temptation and loneliness. Having memorized Bible verses is also useful when you are telling somebody about Jesus.

## Reading Aloud

Finally, try reading the Bible aloud. This is especially profitable:

1. Before or after meals with your family,
2. At small group meetings,
3. At church services, and
4. By yourself

Reading aloud increases your comprehension of the Bible, since now you have not one, but three ways to encounter the Word with your senses:

1. Reading
2. Speaking
3. Listening

As you let the Bible become a regular friend and earpiece into the heart of God, you will find the words of the Psalmist to be true:

"Your word is a lamp to my feet
and a light for my path." (Psalms 119:105)

## Prayer

Father, thank you for giving us the Scriptures. Sometimes they are comforting. Sometimes they make us uncomfortable. Sometimes you speak directly to us with clarity through your Word. Thank you for this gift. Help us to use your gift as it was intended. In Jesus' name, we pray. Amen.

## Participant Guide: 11. Bible—Guidebook for Living

### Memory Verse

"All Scripture is God-breathed and is useful for teaching, rebuking, correcting and training in righteousness, so that the man of God may be thoroughly equipped for every good work." (2 Timothy 3:16-17, NIV)

### Questions and Discussion Points

1. **Read aloud five times** today's memory verse (2 Timothy 3:16-17) and write it on a card.
2. **Discuss.** When we say that the Scripture is inspired, what do we mean?
3. **Discuss.** Have you ever had the Holy Spirit illuminate a verse for you? What was it like?
4. **Activity.** Open your Bible to the Table of Contents. Then open to each of the major sections of the New Testament. Gospels (begins with Matthew), Acts, Paul's Letters (begins with Romans), General Letters (begins with Hebrews), and Revelation. Read a few verses in each section to get the flavor.
5. **Discuss.** What Bible translation do you use? What is the difference between a Bible translation and a Bible paraphrase?
6. **Activity.** Look at the various features of a study Bible. (Mentor: If you don't have one, try to borrow one to bring to the meeting.) Look for scripture cross references, footnotes, a concordance, and other helps.
7. **Your own Bible.** If you don't have your own Bible yet, what is your plan to earn the money to purchase one? What kind would you like to get?
8. **Select** a daily Bible reading plan that seems to suit you and begin to use it this coming week. You can view several Bible reading plans online (www.jesuswalk.com/beginning/bible-reading-plans.htm), then print one out to carry in your Bible.
9. **Review.** Last week we talked about regular giving to God's work on a percentage basis. What plan for regular giving have you decided upon?
10. **Review.** Last week we talked about service to others. In what ways is God using you to serve others?
11. **Review your memory verses** from Lesson 1 (Ephesians 2:8-9), Lesson 2 (John 8:31-32), Lesson 3 (1 John 1:9), Lesson 4 (John 13:34-35), Lesson 5 (1 John 4:7-8), and Lesson 6 (John 3:16), Lesson 7 (John 14:16-17), Lesson 8 (Matthew 5:16), Lesson 9 (Psalms 34:1), and Lesson 10 (Mark 10:45). Try to say them together with your mentor without looking at your cards.
12. **Pray for each other**. Share with your mentor your needs to pray about and ask your mentor how you should pray for him or her. Then spend a few minutes praying for each other aloud and for those to whom you are witnessing.
13. **Appointment**. Set a time and place to meet and go through next week's lesson.

## Outline of Lesson 11. Bible—Guidebook for Living

We have been given powerful aids to help us grow spiritually: Christ's Spirit, Christian brothers and sisters, and the Bible.

1.  **The Inspiration of Scripture**
    - The Bible is inspired by God (2 Timothy 3:16; 2 Peter 1:20-21).
    - The Spirit guided each Bible author to record God's message accurately.
    - Each book of the Bible must be understood within its own culture, historical setting, and language.
    - The Spirit inspired different types of messages God intended for us:
        o  Examples of man's arrogance and disobedience
        o  People of faith to emulate
        o  Songs of praise
        o  Prophecies to correct his people
        o  Letters to guide the early church
    - Because the Bible is inspired, it is speaks with God's authority.

2.  **The Theme of the Bible Is Love**
    - Not primarily a list of laws to obey.
    - The key to understanding the Old and New Testaments is love. The greatest commandments (Matthew 22:37-40): (1) Love God, (2) Love your neighbor.
    - Jesus' teaching is not a heavy burden, but a gentle yoke (Matthew 11:28-30).

3.  **Why We Should Read the Bible**
    - Instruction (John 8:31-32)
    - Correction (Hebrews 4:12)
    - Examples
    - Training and growth
    - Inspiration
    - The Holy Spirit illuminates the Word of God and reveals it to us.

4.  **The New Testaments 27 books and letters have these categories:**
    - Gospels
    - Acts of the Apostles
    - Paul's Letters
    - General Letters
    - Revelation

5.  **Bible translations**
    - Translations from the original language
        o  The Old Testament was written in Hebrew.
        o  The New Testament was written in Greek.
    - Translations vs. paraphrases
        o  Examples of translations: KJV, NIV, NASB, NRSV.

    o  Examples of Paraphrases: Living Bible, The Message.
- A Study Bible contains many resources to help you learn the Bible.

6. **Ways to Read the Bible**
   - A Habit of Daily Bible Reading. Bible reading plans.
     - o New Testament in one chapter a day
     - o Three Bible chapters a day: Psalms, Old Testament, New Testament
     - o Online Bible reading plans to print out and tuck into your Bible
       www.jesuswalk.com/beginning/bible-reading-plans.htm
   - When the Bible seems boring, try making changes—change position, read less, study, reading aloud.
   - Scripture Memory
     - o Write it on a card.
     - o Read it aloud several times.
     - o Try saying from memory.
     - o Review occasionally.
     - o God's word in your heart.
   - Reading aloud
     - o Times to read aloud
       - ▪ Before or after meals with your family
       - ▪ At small group meetings
       - ▪ At church services
       - ▪ By yourself
     - o Reading aloud increases comprehension: reading, speaking, listening.
   - Bible becomes a friend and earpiece to God's heart (Psalm 119:105).

# 12. Lord—Obedient Servants of the King

Being an authentic Christ-follower is much, much more that taking a weekend hike with Jesus. It requires a kind of willing obedience that is foreign to most of us. The relationship with Jesus is complex. It begins with obedience, but concludes with friendship. Let me explain.

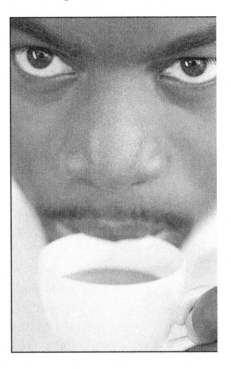

## Follow Me

When Jesus called his first disciples, the command was simple: Follow me!

> "As Jesus was walking beside the Sea of Galilee, he saw two brothers, Simon called Peter and his brother Andrew. They were casting a net into the lake, for they were fishermen. **'Come, follow me,'** Jesus said, 'and I will make you fishers of men.' **At once they left their nets** and followed him." (Matthew 4:18-20)

So the first characteristic of a disciple is one who leaves what he has been doing and follows Jesus wherever he leads.

## Obey Me

But being a disciple goes beyond simple following. It involves obedience, doing what Jesus tells us. Jesus said:

> "If you love me, you will **obey** what I command." (John 14:15)

> "Whoever has my commands and **obeys** them, he is the one who loves me. He who loves me will be loved by my Father, and I too will love him and show myself to him." (John 14:21)

Jesus asked his disciples, "Why do you call me, 'Lord, Lord,' and don't do what I say?" (Luke 6:46). Then he told the Parable of the Wise and Foolish Builders. You may be acquainted with the story. The wise man built his house upon a rock foundation. The foolish man built his house on the sand. All went well until a storm hit. Then the house with no foundation was washed away, but the house built on the rock withstood the flood. Jesus said:

"I will show you what he is like who comes to me and hears my words and **puts them into practice**. He is like a man building a house, who dug down deep and laid the foundation on rock." (Luke 6:47-48)

Many people claim to believe in Jesus, but have no intention of obeying him when it might be inconvenient or conflict with their own will. They have a kind of affection for Jesus, an infatuation, but not real love. Love requires commitment.

## Jesus Demands Priority

Following and obedience are certainly part of a disciple's life. But it goes farther yet. Jesus demands priority over any other kind of allegiance.

"Anyone who loves his father or mother more than me is not worthy of me; anyone who loves his son or daughter more than me is not worthy of me." (Matthew 10:37)

This is a hard saying. The disciples certainly struggled with it—as we must. But Jesus is clear: He demands the highest level of allegiance—greater than family, greater than country.

Why does he demand this? The answer lies in who Jesus is.

## Jesus Is Lord

In Lesson 6 we discussed that Jesus is actually God. He is divine.

Here is a title of Jesus to explore: "Lord." In Greek the word can refer to "owner," as well as to a person in authority: "lord, master."[1] When reverent Jews would read the Old Testament, they would substitute the word "Lord" whenever the name of God ("Yahweh") would appear in the text, so as not to sin by saying the holy name in vain. By New Testament times, the term "Lord," in a religious sense, carries not only the ideas of "owner, lord, and master," but also, "divine Lord, divine Master."

In this light, consider these verses:

"If you confess with your mouth, **'Jesus is Lord,'** and believe in your heart that God raised him from the dead, you will be saved." (Romans 10:9)

"No one can say, **'Jesus is Lord,'** except by the Holy Spirit." (1 Corinthians 12:3)

The statement: "Jesus is Lord!" is the original watchword of the early church, the bedrock of the Christian faith. The question I ask you and ask myself is this: Do the decisions I make reflect that Jesus is *my* Lord? Either he is Lord of every aspect of my life, or I am kidding myself about the depth of my faith and my love for him.

## We Are Servants

Calling Jesus "Lord" means that we honor him and do what he tells us to do. When we call Jesus "Lord," we place ourselves before him as his servants, his willing slaves. As far as

---

[1] *Kurios*, Walter Bauer and Frederick William Danker, *A Greek-English Lexicon of the New Testament and Other Early Christian Literature* (BDAG; Third Edition; based on previous English editions by W.F. Arndt, F.W. Gingrich, and F.W. Danker; University of Chicago Press, 1957, 1979, 2000), p. 577.

the concept of slavery may be from our current culture, that is what the Lord-servant relationship implies.

At the conclusion of Jesus' Parable of the Talents, Jesus tells of the master who rewards his servants for their faithful service:

> "Well done, **good and faithful servant**; you have been faithful over a little, I will set you over much; enter into the joy of your master." (Matthew 25:21, RSV)

These are the words that every disciple longs to hear from Jesus when we finally appear before him. "Well done, good and faithful servant.... Enter into the joy of your master."

## Jesus Is King

Jesus is also called "King." Both the word "Messiah" (Hebrew *māshîaḥ*) and the word "Christ" (Greek *christos*) mean the same thing: literally, "anointed one." In the Old Testament, kings were invested with power when oil was poured out on their head. The king was the anointed one. But Israel's kingdom ended about 587 BC, when the last king was removed from the throne by Babylonian invaders. After that, Israel had been oppressed by foreign powers—most recently the Roman Empire.

But the Jewish people looked forward to the Messiah, the anointed King, who, Scripture promised, would come and restore the Kingdom that God had set up for Israel (the Kingdom of God) and sit enthroned as a victorious King.

Jesus is that King. Jesus is the Christ, the Messiah, the Anointed One who was expected. Imagine how Jesus' preaching must have electrified his audience when he proclaimed,

> "The time has come. The **kingdom of God** is near." (Mark 1:15)

Peter spoke for the rest of the disciples, when he said in awe:

> "You are **the Christ**, the Son of the Living God!" (Matthew 16:16)

When Jesus rode into Jerusalem on Palm Sunday on a donkey, the crowds cried: "Hosanna to the **Son of David**!" (Matthew 21:9). They remembered Israel's great king, David, who was promised that his descendant would be the Messiah.

When Jesus was arrested and interrogated on the charge of claiming to be a king, Pilate asked him: "Are you the **king of the Jews**?" Jesus replied, "Yes, it is as you say." (Mark 15:2). When he was crucified, a placard was nailed to the cross above him that said in three languages: "The **King of the Jews**."

## Humble Yourselves before the King

Jesus is the Messiah, Christ, the King! He is my king and yours. What does it imply about our lives that he is our King and we are his subjects in the Kingdom of God?

It means that we owe him obedience and our highest allegiance. It also means that we are to humble ourselves before him, as subjects do before a great king. The Apostle James teaches:

"Scripture says: 'God opposes the proud but gives grace to the humble.'[2] ... Humble yourselves before the Lord, and he will lift you up." (James 4:6, 10)

In ancient times, people would humble themselves before a king by kneeling before him. That is why we Christians sometimes kneel and bow our heads in reverence before God. But it is more than an outward act. We submit our wills to our King, and say, as Jesus modeled for us, "Not my will, but yours be done" (Luke 22:42).

## A Friend of God

I have tried to illustrate the awesome role of Jesus as divine Lord and King over all. We owe him our very lives. This King laid aside his crown and came to earth to die for his people on the cross, as "a ransom for many" (Mark 10:45).

Because of who he is and what he has done, we understand him to be absolute Lord and absolute King. We are his subjects, his obedient servants.

But now I want to share with you an amazing truth that Jesus told his disciples:

"I no longer call you **servants**, because a servant does not know his master's business. Instead, I have called you **friends**, for everything that I learned from my Father I have made known to you." (John 15:15)

We don't deserve to be friends of Jesus. Certainly none of us—and none of Jesus' original twelve disciples, for that matter—have lived up to his holy standard. Yet he thinks of us disciples, you and me, as his friends.

Yes, it is appropriate that we know him as Lord and Messiah and King, and acknowledge that we are his disciples, servants, and obedient subjects. But he came that we might not just know his power, but also his love—especially his love. That is why he wants to get to know you and for you to get to know him—as a Friend. Jesus wants you as a friend.

That is the message we started with when we began this journey many weeks ago, and that is where I leave you.

God loves you. Jesus loves you. And at very great cost he has forgiven your sin, called you to draw close to him, and desires you to feel his love for you—the love of a friend. He is your friend, and he is one whom I pray you will come to know as your Best Friend.

And now I'll let you go forward on your journey. Jesus is ahead on the path with his hand outstretched to you. "Follow me—friend," he calls.

So go now. Follow Jesus wherever he leads you. Godspeed!

## Prayer

Father, what a privilege I have to know Jesus as King and Lord and God. Humble me. Teach me to be an obedient and faithful servant. And lead me into an intimate friendship with your Son. In Jesus' name, I pray. Amen.

[2] Quoting Proverbs 3:34.

## Participant Guide: 12. Lord—Obedient Servants of the King

### Memory Verse

"Whoever has my commands and obeys them, he is the one who loves me. He who loves me will be loved by my Father, and I too will love him and show myself to him." (John 14:21, NIV)

### Questions and Discussion Points

1. **Read aloud five times** today's memory verse (John 14:21) and write it on a card.
2. **Discuss.** Read the Parable of the Wise and Foolish Builders (Luke 6:46-49). What was Jesus attempting to teach through this parable? What is the point of the parable?
3. **Discuss.** Why is obeying another person so difficult? Why is obeying Jesus so important? Where do you find it most difficult to obey God?
4. **Discuss.** What do we mean when we say: "Jesus is Lord"?
5. **Discuss.** Is the role of being a servant of God demeaning or honorable? What is involved in being a "faithful" servant?
6. **Discuss.** In what sense is Jesus "King"? What are the implications of this?
7. **Discuss.** In John 15:15, Jesus calls his disciples "friends" rather than "servants." Why does he call them friends?
8. **Discuss.** If you are a "friend" of Jesus, what does that mean for your life? What benefits will it bless you with? What responsibilities does it place upon you?
9. **Review.** Have you selected a Bible reading plan yet? Which one? How is it working out for you?
10. **Review your memory verses** from Lesson 1 (Ephesians 2:8-9), Lesson 2 (John 8:31-32), Lesson 3 (1 John 1:9), Lesson 4 (John 13:34-35), Lesson 5 (1 John 4:7-8), and Lesson 6 (John 3:16), Lesson 7 (John 14:16-17), Lesson 8 (Matthew 5:16), Lesson 9 (Psalms 34:1), Lesson 10 (Mark 10:45), and Lesson 11 (2 Timothy 3:16-17). Try to say them together with your mentor without looking at your cards.
11. **Pray for each other**. Share with your mentor your needs to pray about and ask your mentor how you should pray for him or her. Then spend a few minutes praying for each other aloud, and for those to whom you are witnessing.
12. **Select**. Since this series is now over, what kind of Bible study or small group will you become a part of so you can continue studying the Bible with others?

**Please do me a favor – help evaluate the course you've just taken. Go to:**

www.jesuswalk.com/beginning/evaluation.htm

Thank you!

## Outline of Lesson 12. Lord—Obedient Servants of the King

1. **Discipleship Begins with Obedience**
   - Following. Jesus called his disciples, "Come, follow me." (Matthew 4:18-20).
   - Obedience
     o Obedience is a sign of our love for Jesus (John 14:15, 21).
     o The Parable of the Wise and Foolish Builders (Luke 6:47-48) teaches that we must put into practice Jesus' teachings.
   - Priority (Matthew 10:37). Jesus demands our highest level of allegiance.
2. **Obedience Is Required Because of Who Jesus Is**
   - Jesus Is Lord.
     o Implication of his title as "Lord"
       ▪ Means: "owner, lord, master."
       ▪ Lord was substituted for the divine name Yahweh.
       ▪ "Jesus is Lord" means Jesus is our divine Lord and Master.
     o "Jesus is Lord" is the first Christian confession (Romans 10:9; 1 Corinthians 12:3).
     o We are the Lord's servants. Parable of the Talents: "Good and faithful servant" (Matthew 25:21).
   - Jesus Is King
     o Both "Messiah" and "Christ" mean "Anointed One."
     o Kings were anointed with oil when they were crowned.
     o Jesus is the Messiah, the delivering king, who will restore the Kingdom of God (Mark 1:15; Matthew 16:16; Matthew 21:9; Mark 15:2).
     o We must humble ourselves before the King (James 4:6, 10; Luke 22:42).
3. **Jesus Calls Us Friends**
   - Though Jesus is divine Lord and King and Savior, he calls us his friends (John 15:15).
   - Friendship is an expression of his love.
   - God loves you.
   - Calls you on the journey, "Follow me, friend."

# Appendix 1. The Role of the Mentor

The *JesusWalk: Beginning the Journey* series of lessons for new believers is designed around the relationship between the new Christian and a mentor. By mentor I don't mean some highly formal relationship, but, as the dictionary defines the term: "a trusted counselor or guide; tutor, coach."[1]

It is often best if the mentor is nearly the same age as the new believer, or perhaps a few years older. The most important aspect is that the mentor is a healthy, growing Christian himself or herself. The best growth for a new believer is going to be in tandem with a Christian who is a bit more mature in the Lord, one who can lead the way and show the path.

## Qualifications of Mentors

Here's what we are looking for in a mentor. See if this fits you.

**1. Growing in Christ**. No one expects you to be perfect. But it is important that you are growing in Christ. That when the Holy Spirit convicts you of a sin, you quickly repent and ask for forgiveness and cleansing.

**2. Obedient**. You need to be a person who is seeking to be obedient to Christ yourself. That way you can help model obedience.

**3. Quiet time**. It is vital that you take time every day to spend with the Lord, missing only an occasional day. Since this kind of quiet time will be one of the most important factors in helping your new believer grow, you will need to be able to share how this works for you.

**4. Active in a local congregation**. You need to be an active part of a local Christian church. This both enriches your own spiritual life and it enables you to invite and involve your new Christian in the life of the church.

**5. Loving**. As you work with new believers, you will find that there will be significant areas in their lives that are seriously out of line with a Christian lifestyle. You won't approve—I hope! That is to be expected. But if you come across as harsh and judgmental, that won't help, but rather hurt. You need to model the kind of patience, love, and

---

[1] *Merriam-Webster's 11th Collegiate Dictionary.*

forgiveness of Jesus Christ himself. Remember, it is the Holy Spirit who is responsible to change your new believer's life, not you. James instructs us:

> "And the prayer offered in faith will make the sick person well; the Lord will raise him up. If he has sinned, he will be forgiven. Therefore confess your sins to each other and pray for each other so that you may be healed. The prayer of a righteous man is powerful and effective." (James 5:15-16)

Pray diligently and then trust God to work in your new believer's life. God is faithful!

**6. Accountable to your pastor.** It is important that you are in regular touch with your pastor or someone your pastor appoints to oversee your ministry of mentoring and discipling. This will help you gain wisdom, avoid pitfalls, and grow in your own spiritual gifts.

**7. Discreet.** It is vital that your new believer can trust you with the confidential matters of his or her life, without feeling that you will be telling someone else. So you need to keep such matters strictly confidential. If you think, however, that there's a crisis that your new believer needs help with that is beyond you, then get some help from your pastor or a person appointed to help you. Your relationship with your new believer is all about trust.

**8. Same gender.** It is best—unless you are married to your new believer—that the mentor is of the same sex as the new believer. Since the mentor—new believer relationship will be a close one, you don't want the dynamics of sexual attraction getting in the way. Be wise.

**9. Committed.** You will need to be willing to commit yourself to this ministry each week for at least 12 weeks. Don't begin this unless you are willing to do what it takes to finish. Your new Christian is depending upon you.

**10. Watchful and in prayer.** Since you are embarking on a front-line ministry to help someone who has previously been under the enemy's influence, you will be a renewed target for temptation yourself. Be watchful and in prayer.

## You Don't Have to Know Everything

You may be wondering: What if the new Christian asks me a question that I don't know how to answer? You may think you don't know enough about the Bible to do this.

Let me encourage you. The new believer won't expect you to know everything. Just say, "I'll find out about that and then get back to you." Then ask your pastor to help you answer the question and share the answer the next week. You'll learn a lot as you take on this ministry. And you'll know the Bible better when you finish than when you began. It's okay.

If you set yourself up as someone who knows everything, you'll fail. Present yourself as a fellow traveler along the same road, just one who knows the way a little better. You are a guide, but one who looks to the Great Shepherd yourself, just like you are teaching the new believer to do.

## What Is a Mentoring Session Like?

There is no one "right" way to mentor someone. Every situation and personality is different. But the *JesusWalk: Beginning the Journey* series is designed to fit a weekly meeting between you and your new Christian that takes an hour or perhaps a bit longer.

Here is how a typical one hour and fifteen minute mentoring session might take place:

| | |
|---|---|
| 15 min. | **Catching up**. Spend some time talking about how things are going. No rush to get into the lesson. You are building a relationship through which the love of Christ is flowing. |
| 15 min. | **Watch the video**. If you are not able to watch the video (either online or on a DVD), the lessons are available in audio format (MP3) as well as in written form. The lesson material is designed to be watched or read in about 15 minutes. Videos are online at www.jesuswalk.com/beginning/ |
| 30 min. | **Discuss the questions and discussion points**. At the end of each lesson is Participant Guide that includes a list of questions and discussion points for you and your new Christian to discuss. These Participants Guides can be obtained free online. Please print these out before the session—or refer to them in the book version (available at a modest cost). |

www.jesuswalk.com/beginning/beginning-handouts.pdf

Don't do all the talking yourself or answer all the questions. Rather, seek to draw out your new believer and get him or her talking. As he or she struggles to find the answer, major learning is going on. Do not short-circuit that process by prompting or giving an answer too early. Only if he or she can't seem to grasp the point, should you be more direct about the answer.

These questions and discussion points are designed—with the lesson itself—to stimulate Christian growth in your new Christian. There are points for review, for questions about how he or she is doing applying previous lessons, and questions to help your new Christian grasp the new lessons. The discussion points are designed to help your new Christian grasp truth and then apply it in his or her daily life.

| | |
|---|---|
| 5 min. | **Scripture memory**. Spend time with your new Christian seeking to learn the memory verse for the current lesson and reviewing past verses. It is best that you learn these verses, too. Learn them using the Bible translation most often used in your church. |
| 10 min. | **Prayer**. This is a time for you to pray for your new Christian's needs. But just as important, the new Christian will learn to pray for his or her own needs and for yours. Do not be afraid of praying aloud. Christians have been praying for each other aloud for thousands of years. |

1 min.          **Appointment**. Set a time and place for your meeting together next week.

## Where Should You Meet?

Anywhere is fine, so long as you will be able to talk freely:

1.   Coffee shop or restaurant
2.   Apartment, home, or room
3.   Park or square
4.   Internet café or library. You could watch the video there, then go outside to talk.

If you are watching the online video together (recommended), then try to find a location that has Internet access. Other alternatives are to use the DVD (available for purchase) or to download the video onto a computer for later viewing. Or you can download and play the audio (MP3) version or read the lesson together. There's lots of flexibility.

## What Do You Need for the Session?

*   **Computer** (optional). If you're meeting in a place that has Internet access, you can watch the video (or listen to the audio) on a computer at that location or on a laptop that you might bring with you.
*   **Bible**. Bring your Bible with you to each session. If your new Christian doesn't have a Bible yet, bring an extra one for him or her. Later your new Christian may want to purchase a study Bible in a new translation.
*   **Memory Verse, Questions, and Discussion Points**. If you and your new Christian each have a copy of the *JesusWalk: Beginning the Journey* book, then bring that to each session. If not, you may want to print out the online lesson or, at the very least, the two-page handout for that lesson *for each of you*. This can be found online: "Participant Guide: Memory Verses, Questions, and Discussion Points."

    www.jesuswalk.com/beginning/beginning-handouts.pdf
*   **Cards** on which to write the memory verses.
*   **Pen or Pencil** to take notes and write down prayer requests.

## The Importance of Bible Memory

One component of this discipleship curriculum is Scripture memory. This may be familiar to you—or perhaps you have never attempted it. In either case, I want to encourage you to be faithful to work with your new believer to memorize the verses indicated. Why don't you and he or she decide to memorize them together?

I have given the memory verses in the New International Version, but feel free to substitute whatever Bible translation is most used in your congregation. If English is a second language for your new believer, consider learning the verse in his or her native language— the "language of the heart."

Here's what I have found best for Bible memory:

1.   **Write out the verse** on a 3" x 5" card (any size will do).

2. **Read the verse out loud** about five times. Do this together with your new believer. It will help you too.
3. **Say the verse from memory** several times, only looking at the card when you can't remember a word or phrase.
4. **Place the card** where you can see it often—on a mirror, desk, car dashboard, etc.
5. **Review** this memory verse and previous verses regularly.

Scripture memory is work, no doubt about it. But it will pay rewards for a lifetime. The Psalmist said:

"I have hidden your word in my heart
that I might not sin against you." (Psalm 119:11)

It is pretty clear that Jesus and the apostles had committed many Scriptures to memory.

At the end of your session each week, have your new Christian take out his or her memory cards and review the previous weeks' verses, plus trying to learn the new verse. Do this each week and you will be surprised how well you will have learned Scripture.

## The Importance of Your Mentoring Ministry

This mentoring role is an extremely significant ministry. You will be an assistant to the Holy Spirit in beginning to get a new believer started in a healthy way on the journey.

You will find that the relationship you will develop with your new Christian will be precious to you. Years from now you will look back on these twelve weeks and smile from the memories. You will be carrying out your ministry faithfully—and will be blessed immeasurably in the process.

What a privilege you have before you, to be a mentor, a friend, and a fellow traveler on this journey with Christ.

# Appendix 2. For Pastors and Church Leaders

Pastor or church leader, *JesusWalk: Beginning the Journey* is designed to make your job easier. It is my experience that most churches just don't have in place a careful plan to nurture new believers in the very early days of their Christian lives. And most churches don't have enough new believers at any one time to form a class for them.

*JesusWalk: Beginning the Journey* gives you what you need. It is a carefully designed, 12-lesson teaching and discussion curriculum designed to help new believers develop into healthy, growing Christians. It is also available at low or no-cost. All you need to do is give the mentor an Internet web address. He or she can go there, print out the lessons and discussion points, and watch each 15-minute online video lesson with the new believer.

## Costs—Free is Good!

Though people can access this free, you may want to purchase a short book that contains all the lessons for the mentors and new Christians who will be going through this program. There is also a DVD set available so the lessons can be watched by the mentor and new believer—or even a class or group—in locations that don't have Internet access. You can order these materials online if you like (www.jesuswalk.com/books/beginning.htm).

But whether or not your church can afford these tools, they're available free on the Internet. The only cost then is Internet access time and the cost of printing webpages that contain the lessons and questions. Don't let lack of money stand in the way of using this program.

## The Pastor's Role

Here's how this might work for the pastor and your congregation. After a person becomes a Christian, as pastor or a leader delegated to this ministry:

1.  You **assign** a mentor to each new believer. The mentor should be a growing Christian of the same gender as the new believer, who can spend an hour or hour and a half with him or her each week. It is best if the age of the mentor and new believer are similar, though that is not absolutely necessary. The mentor could well be the person

who led the new believer to Christ. The mentor needs to be someone who is currently growing well in Christ, but he or she does not need to be fully mature.

2.  You **train** the mentor by watching the mentor training video or reading together—Appendix 1: "The Role of the Mentor." Then go over with him or her what will be expected and how to approach this ministry.

3.  You **send out** the mentor to make an appointment and then meet with the new believer. Encourage the mentor to meet in a relaxed setting, perhaps a coffee shop or Internet café or in a home, to watch the video lesson or read the lesson together, and then talk about it using the included discussion points.

4.  You **monitor** the progress of discipling by staying in touch with the mentor regularly. Since this may stretch the mentor beyond his or her comfort zone, this can be a good time to mentor the mentor and help this ministry be a growth opportunity for him or her.

5.  You **meet with** the mentor and new believer, but only occasionally as needed. If you are present very often, you will suppress the mentor's own developing gift of ministry. But the mentor might need some help with Lesson 7. Holy Spirit—The Power of God's Presence," that discusses the Spirit-led life. If you think it is necessary, watch the lesson 7 video with them, then help them through the discussion questions.

6.  You **celebrate** the new believer's progress. This curriculum does not assume that the new believer grew up in the church, so it starts from the very basics. It encourages the mentor and new believer to contact the pastor regarding baptism and church membership, so you can celebrate new life in Christ publically with the new believers in the way that your church does these things.

Pastor, you may be tempted to do the mentoring yourself. After all, you may have better training and are deeper in the Lord than nearly anyone else in the congregation. I encourage you to resist that temptation. Rather, prayerfully find a possible mentor and then extend your ministry through him or her. In doing this you are fulfilling your Scriptural mandate "to equip the saints for the work of ministry" (Ephesians 4:12, NRSV). As you do this, your congregation will be able to grow naturally through the leaders you are developing.

## Doctrine: A Trans-Denominational Approach

As a pastor or church leader you are rightly concerned about the doctrines that your people will be exposed to. *JesusWalk: Beginning the Journey* is designed to be a tool that can be trusted and used by any denomination.

This material doesn't shy away from the hard issues of serving Christ as a disciple. We consider sin, repentance, commitment, salvation, resisting temptation, enduring persecution, practicing Christian love, giving to God's work, serving one another, and living by the Spirit.

However, I go out of my way to present this material without discussing them in ways that offend particular teachings of Christian denominations. For example:

- **Baptism** is strongly encouraged in Lesson 1. Rescue—Grace and Forgiveness, but we don't specify the mode of baptism. Instead, new believers are referred to churches to explain the details. Since I am assuming that the new believers have no church background, I haven't touched on the issue of infant baptism or "re-baptism." Pastors can explain these matters where appropriate.
- **Church membership** is strongly encouraged in Lesson 4. Fellowship—Connecting to a Community of Christians, but we leave it to pastors and churches to fill in the details for the new believer.
- The **Lord's Supper** is mentioned in Lesson 6. Gospel—Understanding Christ's Story, without being specific about how it is to be administered. Your church traditions regarding the Eucharist are honored, not undermined.
- A **Spirit-led Christian life** is taught in Lesson 7. Holy Spirit—The Power of God's Presence. We don't use explicit Pentecostal terminology, though most Pentecostal and non-Pentecostal groups should be comfortable with this teaching on the Spirit-led life.
- **Spiritual gift examples** given are both "natural" and "supernatural," though this is presented in a non-controversial manner. Speaking in tongues is not specifically mentioned.
- The **authority of Scripture** is assumed throughout and discussed explicitly in Lesson 11. Bible—Our Guidebook for Living, though we don't treat the issue of inerrancy. We leave that to you.

This does not mean that I don't have clear views on these subjects. I discuss controversial issues in my in-depth Bible studies as they appear in the text. The purpose of *JesusWalk: Beginning the Journey*, however, is not to generate controversy, but to make a high quality spiritual formation and discipleship tool available to the greatest possible number of Christian churches at the lowest possible price—free.

As important as sound doctrine is, however, the purpose of *JesusWalk: Beginning the Journey* is not solely doctrinal. This series aims at solid, practical Christian living. The purpose is to develop in new believers a healthy Christian approach to life and to help them develop spiritual disciplines that will allow them to continue to grow well in the Lord long after they complete this series.

## Use in Classes or Small Groups

This series is specifically designed to be used with a new believer and a mentor. However, it is adaptable for use with a mentor who works with two or even three new believers at a time. What you gain is increased "efficiency" of ministry personnel. What you lose, at some point, however, is the personal mentoring presence. I believe it is vital for the new believer to observe a growing Christian up close so that he or she is able to serve as a model for growth.

If your class or small group has already been living the Christian life for some time, this is not the series for you. You need discipleship curricula that does not assume a complete lack of knowledge about Christianity. Instead, you need Bible studies that are more intensive and are appropriate for more mature Christians.

However, if you are working with a group of new believers who are pretty much at the same point in their early spiritual growth, this curriculum could work for a class—and you could use it with a mixed group of both men and women.

You might watch the video together. Secure the DVD set for your church and supply the book for each person—mentor and new believer alike. Or print out a copy of the two-page lesson handout for each participant. Then break into two smaller sub-groups—men with men, women with women—to talk through the discussion points together.

Since the discussion points are designed to instill individual accountability and follow-through, make sure that your discussion groups are *very* small. I recommend an absolute *maximum* of three new believers for each mentor. It is best for a mentor to stay with the same group of new believers through the entire series.

If you decide on a group approach, you will want to train the mentors to work together as a discipling team. You might have the mentors come 15 minutes early for prayer and meet together once or twice during the series for instruction and guidance in their ministry.

That's the overview. I hope you'll be able to use *JesusWalk: Beginning the Journey* in your church in order to bring fruit to maturity for the Kingdom.

# Appendix 3. How to Select a Bible

One task of a new Christian is to obtain a Bible. But which Bible is best? Which translation? Should you pay extra to get a study Bible?

Let's look at some of the factors you should be aware of in selecting a Bible.

## Translation Approaches

You know, of course, that the Bible was not written in English, but in Hebrew (and a bit of Aramaic) in the Old Testament and Greek in the New Testament. A translation tries to render the original language into clear, accurate English. There are two types of translations:

1. **Literal word-for-word translation**. This makes for accuracy, but can be rather wooden to read out loud. A good example of this type is the New American Standard Bible.

2. **Dynamic thought-for-thought correspondence**. Here the translator takes a thought in the original language and tries to translate it into the same concept in good English, without being tied to the exact words in the original. A good example of this might be *Today's English Version* (TEV).

The best Bible for general use contains a balance of both. You want a careful, accurate translation, but one that reads easily and clearly for family devotions or public worship.

Another issue is the underlying Greek and Hebrew text. The KJV translators worked with the best texts available to them in 1611, but in the last 150 years we have gained a much more accurate understanding of what the original text must have been. Nearly all modern translations are enriched by the translators working from the most accurate Greek and Hebrew texts possible.

## English Translations

Here are some of the most popular English translations. Your church or tradition may have a particular preference, but any one of these might be a good choice for you:

- **The King James Version** (KJV, 1611) is, of course, the granddaddy of our English Bibles. For its day, it was a very accurate translation and is still used in many congregations today. In 1984, the **New King James Version** (NKJV) was published by Thomas Nelson. Translators modernized the language of archaic words substantially and removed most of the "thees" and "thous." The underlying Greek and Hebrew texts remained the same as the KJV of 1611. For churches with a strong King James tradition, the NKJV is a popular alternative.

- **The New International Version** (NIV) was first translated by evangelical scholars in 1973, with revisions in 1983 and 1988. It is an excellent balance between readability and accuracy of translation. For years it has been the most popular newer translation in the United States, especially among evangelical churches.

- **New American Standard Bible** (NASB or NASV), translated by the Lockman Foundation, was published in 1971 and revised in 1977. Its big strength is its consistency in literally translating words and tenses. It is known as a very accurate translation, though perhaps not as easy to read aloud as some others.

- **New Revised Standard Version** (NRSV, 1989) and its predecessor, the Revised Standard Version (RSV, 1952), are careful translations in the King James tradition. Several Protestant denominations prefer the NRSV. It is both accurate and readable.

Of course there are many other modern translations, many of them good for serious Bible study, too numerous to list here. The original *Living Bible* and *The Message* are not translations, but paraphrases. They can be refreshing to read, but aren't good Bibles for careful study.

## Study Bibles

After you have decided what translation to use, I encourage you to purchase a study Bible, since it will contain a number of tools in one volume that can help you dig deeper. Nearly every Bible publisher offers a study Bible. Your local Christian bookstore can help you figure out which one is right for you. Here are some of the features that you will come to appreciate:

- **Cross References.** In a column next to the text, a study Bible lists several other verses with a similar idea or theme. For example, for "Nicodemus" in John 3:1, my Bible refers me to John 7:50 and 19:39 where he appears again. For "Rabbi" in verse 2, the cross references send me to Matthew 23:7 which has nine more references on this topic that I can explore. These cross references won't be comprehensive, but will point out the main passages that discuss any related ideas.

- **Bible Book Introductions.** It is important to know something about the author, date, themes, circumstances, and intended audience of the Bible book or letter you are studying. In most study Bibles you will find one to three pages of introductory comments for each book with a brief outline.

- **Study Notes or Annotations.** Study Bibles have footnotes at the bottom of the page to help explain some of the more obscure ideas you will run across—a kind of mini-commentary. Remember, these aren't part of the Bible itself, but can often point you in the right direction in your study. These notes are usually indexed for easy reference.

- **Concordance.** You have had a verse on the tip of your tongue, but don't know exactly where it is. A concordance helps you find a Bible passage if you can think of a key word or two that the verse contains. A concordance can also help you find other verses that teach a concept or use a word found in the passage you are studying.
- **Topical Index.** In addition to a concordance, some study Bibles have a separate topical index that helps you find scripture references on a particular topic.
- **Maps.** Part of understanding what is happening in narrative passages of Scripture is learning the geography, the location of cities, battles, mountains, valleys, enemies, etc.

Other features you may find include articles on various topics, a brief Bible dictionary, outlines of topics and Bible books, index of place names, time lines, and so on.

Now you know enough to select a Bible that is right for you. Go get a great one and read it for the rest of your life!

# Appendix 4. Discipleship Resources

There are many resources available for those who seek to develop a ministry in discipling believers. Beginning during World War II, the Navigators pioneered this type of ministry and have contributed much expertise to the Body of Christ. These are some of the resources I have found especially helpful.

LeRoy Eims, *The Lost Art of Disciple Making* (Zondervan, 1978, ISBN 031037281X). This is a classic. One of the most helpful features is Appendix 1, "Training Objectives for a Disciple," a careful listing of 30 discipleship topics, each with a one-sentence objective, activities, materials, and appropriate scriptures. It's worth the price of the book. Used copies are available on Amazon at very low cost.

*Discipleship Journal* is published by NavPress online only. It contains articles on growing in your own spiritual life as well as helping others grow. Excellent. Many back issues are available online for viewing or purchase.

*The Topical Memory System* (NavPress, 2006, ISBN 1576839974), is a classic approach to memorizing 60 important verses. I strongly recommend it.

Bill Hull, *The Complete Book of Discipleship: On Being and Making Followers of Christ* (NavPress, 2006, ISBN 1576838978). This author also wrote the influential *Disciple-Making Pastor* (Baker, 2007, ISBN 0801066220) and *The Disciple-Making Church* (Revell, 1998, ISBN 0800756274

CPSIA information can be obtained
at www.ICGtesting.com
Printed in the USA
BVOW09s0857200318

510799BV00003B/44/P